"We all need to build our own toolkits for better professional performance and deepen our life satisfaction. Antonia has given us a comprehensive, masterful playbook to help us on this journey."

—Khe Hy,
Founder and CEO of RadReads

"Thank you, Antonia Bowring. This book is a labor of love and it contains so much of your executive coaching expertise, and is so accessible and practical. Anyone who buys this book can put these coaching frameworks into action and they will see an immediate impact in how they show up at work and in the rest of life."

—Pat Mitchell,
Cofounder, ConnectedWomenLeaders;
Editorial Director, TEDWomen, and Author of
Becoming a Dangerous Woman: Embracing Risk to Change the World

"If you are struggling to manage your ADHD symptoms, then you should put this book on your reading list. It's a game-changer! It completely opened my eyes to what was possible as an adult living with ADHD. A lot of self-help books give advice on how to change certain areas of your life, but they don't address the habits and patterns that are likely to creep back in and ruin your progress. This one does! Thank you, Antonia, I'm recommending it to everyone!"

—Andrew Fingerman,
CEO Photoshelter

COACH YOURSELF!

ANTONIA BOWRING

COACH YOURSELF!

INCREASE
AWARENESS,
CHANGE BEHAVIOR,
AND **THRIVE**

WILEY

Published by John Wiley & Sons, Inc., Hoboken, New Jersey.
Published simultaneously in Canada.

For general information on our other products and services or for technical support, please
contact our Customer Care Department within the United States at (800) 762-2974, outside
the United States at (317) 572-3993 or fax (317) 572-4002.

Wiley also publishes its books in a variety of electronic formats. Some content that appears in
print may not be available in electronic formats. For more information about Wiley products,
visit our web site at www.wiley.com.

Library of Congress Cataloging-in-Publication Data:

Names: Bowring, Antonia, author.
Title: Coach yourself! : increase awareness, change behavior, and thrive /
  Antonia Bowring.
Description: First edition. | Hoboken, New Jersey : Wiley, 2023. |
  Includes index.
Identifiers: LCCN 2023008787 (print) | LCCN 2023008788 (ebook) | ISBN
  9781119931454 (hardback) | ISBN 9781119931478 (adobe pdf) | ISBN
  9781119931461 (epub)
Subjects: LCSH: Executive coaching. | Mindfulness (Psychology) |
  Organizational behavior. | Success in business.
Classification: LCC HF5549.5.C53 B689 2023 (print) | LCC HF5549.5.C53
  (ebook) | DDC 658.4/07124—dc23/eng/20230316
LC record available at https://lccn.loc.gov/2023008787
LC ebook record available at https://lccn.loc.gov/2023008788

Cover Design: Wiley
Cover Image: © antishock/Getty Images

SKY10052732_080723

Between stimulus and response, there is a space and in that space lies our power to choose and in our choice lies our growth and freedom.

—Victor Frankel

I merely took the energy it takes to pout and wrote some blues.

—Duke Ellington

Contents

Introduction: Preparing for the Journey

"Life is a journey, not a destination."

—Ralph Waldo Emerson

A couple of years ago, I called my coaching colleague, Lisa, to ask her advice.

"Lisa," I said, "I feel like it's time for me to work with a coach again, is there anyone you'd recommend?"

"If someone asked me to refer them to a master coach, I'd recommend you," she said. "And besides, can't you coach yourself with the frameworks you use with your clients?"

I was shocked by her response. Is that me she's talking about? I didn't consider myself to be a master coach, but I felt incredibly validated hearing her refer to me that way. (Yes, coaches can have moments of imposter syndrome, too!)

I am passionate about what coaching can do and that exchange with Lisa got me thinking about how to spread what I knew about coaching with others.

I realized I rely on certain "go-to" coaching frameworks when I hit bumps in the road—ranging from small speed bumps to major obstacles that require a metaphorical four-wheel all-terrain vehicle to overcome. My recent bumps have ranged from needing to develop better communication skills with my teenage sons to grappling with my adult ADHD diagnosis.

After receiving my diagnosis, I found it challenging at first to apply the label of ADHD to myself although I immediately felt a sense of relief: "Oh, so that's what's going on. . . . It's not just that I lack self-control." It also became the catalyst for me to write this book.

A great deal of my journey in accepting my ADHD was about reframing how I saw myself: building new awareness of my strengths and challenges, and using coaching frameworks as additional scaffolding in my work and personal life.

I started cataloging my favorite coaching frameworks, specifically the ones that had brought the most success to my coaching clients and me. That led to my decision to write this book: I wanted to share these powerful tools to help people become more effective leaders, better parents, and ultimately happier and more accomplished people who are successfully living up to their potential.

In this book, I detail the knowledge and experience I have gained from a decade as a coach, and two decades as management consultant and in the C-suite. These frameworks and tactics will help you be a more empathetic, realistic, and effective coach to yourself. This book will help you lead by example as you employ the practices described here with your clients, colleagues, family members, friends, and romantic partners!

Your Journey of Self-Discovery

If you are reading this book, you are a motivated learner and already on a journey of self-discovery. You want change and progress, and you want to harness your gifts and strengths in new ways. This book will teach you more about yourself and help you acquire tools to be more successful at work and at home. Keep in mind these three "Ps" as you move through the book:

- Practice – these frameworks require practice to implement them well.

- Patience – be kind to yourself and recognize you are on a journey. Moving in the right direction of real change and staying the course, even when it's challenging, is success in and of itself.
- Party – celebrate along the way. This is a joyful learning journey that benefits from positive reinforcement.

My Journey of Self-Discovery

Before I became a coach, my education included one undergraduate degree and two masters; and my 20-plus-year career spanned Canadian politics and international economic development to management consulting and female founder start-ups. I pivoted from the C-suite to coaching full time 10 years ago and never looked back.

I see now how my work experience helped prepare me to be an executive coach. I confronted a number of challenges during my career without the benefit of a coach, and I could have used one! I also could have used more strategic career guidance along the way.

- Managing up was a big challenge, especially early in my career when I worked across cultures with founders much older than me. I needed help to learn the best strategies to influence and persuade, and how to balance respect for them and their views with the work goals I was accountable for. Later I worked as COO at an organization where I had two bosses, and successfully managing up was complex and critical to my ability to do my job well.
- Getting fired was a deeply humbling experience. When the new president of the foundation where I was working told me that I was being let go, it was a tremendous blow to my ego and my confidence. I remember thinking, "I don't get

fired. I get promoted! How can this be happening to me, I thought I was a winner?"

- I also wasted years not doing the work I was born to do (coaching). For years I kept thinking I needed more credentials to be qualified enough and I undersold my skills. It took me too long to fully tap into my interests and strengths, and I often doubted my expertise. My level of confidence varied; I usually felt I was only as good as the client presentation I'd just made or the last deal I'd negotiated.

The humility I learned, the empathy I developed, and, ironically, the confidence I ended up having in my judgment were all benefits of going through experiences like these. That said, I needed time to hone my perspective, but I could have accelerated the learning, insights, and subsequent positive actions if I'd had the benefit of working with a good coach.

This is what inspires me to be in service to others. Of course, you have to learn your own lessons and forge your own pathway, but a coach can help you move through this process faster.

I wake up every morning feeling blessed and privileged to do this work. I get to support people who want to understand themselves better and take actions based on their new insights and new self-perceptions. Many of my clients have achieved goals they never thought possible, just by making small changes in their behavior and making sure those changes stick. This book will help you make changes too.

Call to Action

Why am I inspired to share these coaching frameworks with you? In three words: these frameworks work. And this book will help you master them. This isn't a book you have to start at the beginning and read to the conclusion. I think of it as a very friendly reference book. Pick it up and start with a chapter that speaks to you. Where are you challenged right now? Is it having tough conversations? Then you'll want to hone in on Part III, which is all about communication frameworks. Managing a team? Part IV covers individual management skills and team dynamics. Over the past 10 years, I have employed every one of these frameworks with dozens and dozens of clients. They all work.

You will need to adapt these frameworks to your specific needs and your learning style, and, of course, you will need to keep your organization's culture in mind too.[1]

And if you have a diagnosis of ADHD, you will find the frameworks in this book extremely helpful in times of need. It's simple: people with ADHD often require more scaffolding to be productive and efficient, and this book provides it.

The insights I provide on active listening and suggested open-ended questions in Chapter 8 resonate with many ADHD clients since sometimes they feel uncomfortable in meetings interacting with colleagues, and are looking for hacks to make it less awkward. I end the book with a section dedicated to helping you maintain your coaching wins. Once you have developed more awareness and shifted behaviors, what support do you need to avoid regressing to prior behaviors you worked hard to change?

I am so glad to be going on this journey with you.

Launching the Journey

In Chapter 1, I review some of the basics about what executive coaching is (and is not), and why it has experienced such growth in the past two decades. I then describe my coaching philosophy and coaching process in Chapter 2. I wrote Chapter 3 specifically for my readers with ADHD and it includes a framework for living successfully with ADHD. Finally, I share my thoughts on how to navigate the rest of the book in Chapter 4.

1

The Executive Coaching Context

Success is not final, failure is not fatal: it is the courage to continue that counts

—Winston Churchill

What Is Executive Coaching?

In the most basic (and driest) terms, "executive coaching is a regular one-on-one development process designed to produce positive changes in business behavior in a limited time frame."[1] Building from there, when I am hired as an executive coach, I serve as a professional reframer, cheerleader, sounding board, and accountability partner to my client. I help you develop awareness about yourself, help you unearth your challenges, and create actionable goals related to them, and then hold you accountable for achieving those goals. And the ideal result is an improved situation where you thrive (and if you lead a team, it will thrive, too).

Coaching isn't therapy because the focus is forward looking, not backward, and is strongly focused on action and results, rather than unearthing the reasons for past and present behaviors. Coaching isn't consulting either because a coach is not telling you what to do, or even making strong recommendations about what you should do, which we expect from consultants.

The essence of coaching is that we all have the answers inside ourselves, and the role of the coach is to help us access our own answers by shifting perspectives, developing new insights and strategies, and accessing new resources.

Executive coaching is different from life coaching. Life coaching helps people attain greater fulfillment with an emphasis on their life goals, relationships, and day-to-day lives.[2] Executive coaching is more focused on the work environment and business results, but it also incorporates elements of life coaching since we can't (and shouldn't) separate the "rest of our lives" from our "work lives."

Why Is Executive Coaching So Popular?

In an increasingly complex and competitive global economy, businesses and organizations of all sizes are looking for ways to differentiate their brands and enhance their value propositions. Enlightened organizations realize that maintaining a strong cadre of motivated managers and leaders is critical to their bottom-line success. Executive coaching empowers individuals, which, in turn, positively impacts the bottom line.

I believe the enormous growth in coaching is based on several linked factors:

- Information bombards us daily and the pace of change keeps accelerating. Coaches help curate a professional development journey that helps leaders better handle the complexities and keep pace with acceleration.
- Demands on us to perform underscore the need for us all to cultivate external perspectives—good coaches are a combination of cheerleader, truth-teller, and professional reframer. In his TED Talk, surgeon and bestselling author Atul Gawande speaks

eloquently about the power of and need for coaching to become your most successful self.

Great coaches are your external eyes and ears, providing a more accurate picture of your reality. They are breaking your actions down and helping you build them back up again.[3]

- Professional sports teams and athletes have long invested in coaches for support in a variety of ways, from technical skills to strength training to motivation and mindset. Teams and athletes use coaches to achieve success and then maintain it. Why should it be different for companies and individuals?
- Companies recognize that coaching is a perk for executives and is now seen as an integral part of the full compensation package.
- Finally, development conversations that used to be handled by mentors, managers, and elders are today outsourced to coaches. On the one hand that is bad news since it's a reflection of how little time we have available to help others. On the other hand, certified coaches have powerful toolkits to help develop leaders and managers.

The statistics speak for themselves.

- Of individuals and companies who hire a coach, 99% are "satisfied or very satisfied" and 96% say they would repeat the process. For people who receive coaching, 80% report increased self-confidence,[4] and more than 70% reported benefits from improved work performance, relationships, and more effective communication skills.[5]
- Companies investing in coaching also are satisfied: 86% report they recouped their investment on coaching and more, with a median ROI of 7x the investment.[6]
- For companies with a strong coaching culture, 51% report higher revenue than their industry peer group[7] and a 52% reduction in employee burnout.[8]

- In a case study of women leaders who participated in coaching, 75% say the value of executive and leadership coaching is "considerably greater" or "far greater" than the money and time invested.[9]
- One in six entrepreneurs turns to coaching to improve their performance.[10]

It's easy to see why business coaching has moved from a niche area at the turn of this century to a $14.2 billion business in the United States in 2022.[11]

Who Is Executive Coaching For?

Coaching often is associated with assistance for C-suite executives grappling with top-level strategy and leadership issues. Coaching also is valuable for managers, candidates for promotion, or those who have been recently promoted, since their management and leadership skills frequently need enhancing. Founders of early-stage and high-growth companies also invest in coaching, often because of the pressures from scaling up a business and the loneliness many of them encounter. And some individuals are so invested in their own development that they seek out and pay for their own coach, typically when someone is looking to make a career transition.

Executive coaching covers a wide range of issues, including strategy, delegation, effective listening, collaboration with peers, executive presence, presentation and communication skills, hiring practices, negotiating contracts, and team management. In essence, coaching addresses issues that get in the way of the client being the best business leader and people manager that they can be.

Coaching can be profoundly transformational when clients tap into sources of confidence and strength that enable them to live their truth and purpose as leaders and humans. At the transactional level, clients gain new behaviors from coaching that help them to thrive more. At the other extreme, insights from coaching can transform their lives.

How Do You Know If You Need an Executive Coach?

Generally speaking, no one seeks coaching if everything is going swimmingly in their personal and professional lives. We seek out coaching when we experience a pain point. That is what motivates us to make a change. To be clear, I also coach some leaders who want a coach as a sounding board, and who are committed to lifelong learning and self-development. But generally speaking, I get calls when issues need to be addressed.

Any of the following—alone or in combination—can lead to the decision to explore coaching: issues raised in a performance review, repeated feedback about the same issues and behaviors, 360 review results, personality test results, insights from your boss/peers/direct reports, feedback from family and friends, your gut telling you to get support. Sometimes it's the individual who recognizes the need, sometimes it's the employer, sometimes both.[12]

This book is for anyone who seeks positive change. **To benefit from this book, you need one thing: the desire to invest in yourself and your progress as a professional and as a human being.**

My Coaching Philosophy and Process

What got you here won't get you there.

—Marshall Goldsmith

My coaching philosophy and coaching process are integrated and mutually reinforcing.

My Coaching Philosophy: Motivated and Sustainable Change

*I believe **motivated** people are capable of **abundant learning** and **development**.*

*I **navigate** with my clients through purposeful conversations to support them in:*

- *exploring their **challenges and opportunities**, and clarifying their **goals.***
- ***assessing behaviors**, skills and values.*
- *exploring their goals and options.*
- *building their **plan for change**.*

- *taking **actions**, gaining feedback, trying again.*
- *holding themselves **accountable** for achieving tangible and **sustainable outcomes**.*

Sometimes a prospective client will ask me about my coaching philosophy. The preceding is it in a nutshell—super practical, actionable, and with heavy emphasis on accountability to the process and the results. While my philosophy is not tied to a specific ideology, I ground my approach in positive psychology: "a scientific approach to studying human thoughts, feelings, and behavior, with a focus on strengths instead of weaknesses, building the good in life instead of repairing the bad, and taking the lives of average people up to 'great' instead of focusing solely on moving those who are struggling up to 'normal'.[1] Martin Seligman is considered the founder of positive psychology and his work has been extremely influential in promoting an emphasis on strengths rather than on deficits in coaching.[2]

I have gravitated to this positive psychology perspective because I find many of my clients arrive to work with me, focused on what is "wrong." They feel more empowered and motivated, and even relieved, when we start by looking at their strengths and how to build on them or make adjustments when they are over-leveraged. Research shows that knowing and using your character strengths can help you to better manage stress, achieve your goals, boost your general well-being and discover greater life purpose.[3]

For me, executive coaching is closely linked to business results and my client's personal growth as a result of the coaching engagement. In other words, I want us to see the success of our work in measurable quantifiable outcomes. And that is the result of my client reframing problematic personal narratives, expanding their toolkit to handle challenges better, changing what they put into action to effect change, and having others perceive them differently and in a more productive light as a result of their behavioral shifts.

My Coaching Process

My coaching process (Figure 2.1) is very straightforward and simple but not simplistic! It starts with two key building blocks: a **motivated client** and a trusting, honest **relationship between the client and me**. Establishing clear intentions and then achievable but ambitious **goals** is the first step, and critical to the success of the engagement because it ensures accountability of the coaching process. In the corporate context, goals are frequently subject to a **reality check** that may involve collecting perspectives through 360 reviews and/or the completion of personality assessments.

The next phase involves exploration of the various **options** available to achieve the goal. This is an iterative process: step goals, action items, and anticipated results are captured in an action plan that my client and I create during the engagement. The completed action plan represents the **way forward** that the client has crafted to change and memorialize specific behaviors and attitudes.

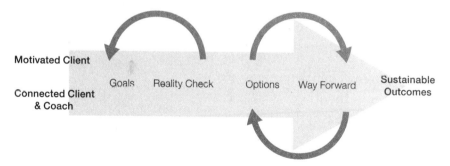

Figure 2.1 Coaching Process.

At the end of the engagement, the client will be on their way to achieve **sustainable outcomes**: specifically, increased awareness about concrete behaviors, practical strategies for changing them, and new behaviors to call upon when faced with similar challenges in the future. The completed action plan is their personal guide to sustainable change.

A typical corporate executive coaching engagement lasts approximately six months. However, I also work with some clients for several years, sometimes with breaks along the way. The latter is more typical of my work with founders and leaders of early-stage, high-growth private companies.

As You Embark on Your Journey

Of course, this experience is different. You are reading a book and don't have direct access to me like my clients do. At the same time, you can gain many insights and make real progress by coaching yourself and rereading parts of this book when challenges arise.

Here are some suggestions for adapting the coaching process for you to be your own coach:

- Collect different perspectives. The easiest way to do this is to ask your colleagues, friends, and family for their insights. Try and vary your questions between ones that require specific responses, such as "How would you describe my communication style?" to more open-ended ones like "What are my superpowers? and "How have you seen me use them well and/or overuse them?"
- Take an online assessment such as Strengthfinders,[4] which comes with a guide for understanding your results. This could help you to formulate your coaching goals.
- Collaborate with friends or colleagues on this journey of self-discovery and goal attainment. You could work as a pair,

or even better, consider forming your own coaching group. An ideal number would be three to five members. This creates automatic accountability and helps on the motivation front, too. You also may want to consider reading this book in an existing book club to maximize group support.

- Implement scaffolding. If you are going to work through this book alone, one strategy to stay on track is to calendar the time you plan to spend on this book and its reflection questions and exercises. By doing so, you are much more likely to sit down with it and coach yourself!

Reflection Questions

- How ready are you to coach yourself because you have hit a bump in the road and need support? On a scale of 1 to 4 (1 – curious but not motivated; 2 – somewhat motivated; 3 – motivated; 4 – VERY motivated)
  - If you answered 1 or 2, I suggest reading Parts I and II of this book to see if that increases your motivation.
  - If you answered 3 or 4, I suggest reading Part I and then digging into the part of the book that most speaks to you and the bump in the road that you are currently navigating. For instance, if you are having challenges managing a team, I'd start with Part IV; if you are procrastinating on a conversation that you need to have but don't want to have, I'd suggest starting with the COIN Framework in Part III.
- How can you gain additional perspectives on your behavior and your situation?
- Are you prepared for this journey? Are you able to schedule time on your calendar to read this book and do some of its exercises? Are you thinking about finding a friend to go through the process with you?

Resources

- "Should You Invest in a Coach?" by Antonia Bowring, Forbes Coaches Council (October 2022). This article highlights Andy Dunn's and Atul Gawande's arguments about the benefits of coaching. (https://www.forbes.com/sites/forbescoaches council/2022/10/21/should-you-invest-in-a-coach/?sh=9cc 4a853a43a)
- *Authentic Happiness* by Martin E. P. Seligman, Simon & Schuster (2002). This book helped promote positive psychology, which has had an enormous impact on the coaching field. The message that we can cultivate happiness by leveraging our strengths remains a highly empowering one.
- *Coach the Person Not the Problem: A Guide to Using Reflective Inquiry* by Dr. Marcia Reynolds , Berrett-Koehler Publishers, Inc. (2020). This is an easy to access coaching primer. It is practical and provides lots of coaching tips and tactics. I love her mantra (and title) "coach the person not the problem."

3

For My Readers with ADHD

It takes courage to grow up and turn out to be who you really are.

—e.e. cummings

My adult diagnosis of ADHD was one of the biggest bumps I've encountered in my adult life and yet it also became the catalyst for me to write this book.

The ADHD definition I use is "a disorder marked by an ongoing pattern of inattention and/or hyperactivity-impulsivity that interferes with functioning or development."[1] Medical professionals stress: ADHD has a strong hereditary component; the onset of ADHD symptoms is traced back to childhood; ADHD symptoms occur across multiple settings, including work, home, and one's social world.[2]

The challenges of recognizing ADHD start with the fact that it can show up with different challenges for someone who has inattentive symptoms (e.g., not listening when spoken to directly) and someone who has hyperactive symptoms (e.g., be constantly in motion or on the go). And some folks display symptoms of both.

In my coaching practice, I use these three buckets to categorize adult ADHD symptoms.

Attention/Focus	Organization/ Prioritization	Emotional Regulation
Failure to give attention to detail	Difficulty organizing tasks	Blurts out
Difficulty sustaining attention	Loses things	Difficulty waiting turn
Difficulty engaging in leisure activities	Difficulty breaking a big goal into subgoals and steps	Low frustration tolerance
Doesn't seem to listen	Failure to give attention to detail	Feels restless
Avoids tasks requiring sustained mental effort	No follow through	Fidgets/taps

Those of us with ADHD need more scaffolding to focus, prioritize, and regulate our emotions. This scaffolding can include anything from a simple wall calendar, an app for accountability, to the frameworks in this book. Frameworks have helped me organize my thoughts, develop strategies for managing my communications and emotions, and process workplace and homelife challenges.

The key message I want you to walk away with is this: attention-deficit/hyperactivity disorder (ADHD) is a diagnosis of one type of neurodiversity. ADHD isn't good or bad, it just is. It is a manifestation of your neurological wiring. It is an aspect of who you are that makes you unique. ADHD can deliver benefits and challenges, similar to other defining characteristics such as deficient color vision, or Asperger syndrome, now part of the larger developmental disorder category of autism spectrum disorder (ASD).[3] What matters is how you think about it, and the self-narrative you tell yourself and communicate to the rest of the world.

Think of the frameworks in this book as scaffolding options available to you. You, the reader with ADHD, decide what resonates, what is valuable, and what you want to try out. And what resonates for a neuro-typical person may be different from what resonates for someone with ADHD. For instance, a neuro-typical person may read this chapter once and absorb everything, while someone with ADHD may need to read it several times to achieve the same level of comprehension. That is the value of this book: it is flexible and if you are curious, you can learn strategies and tactics to enhance your personal and professional development journey, whether or not you have ADHD.

Recognition, Acceptance, Education, and Integration

As a coach, I emphasize the following four concepts to anyone on the journey to make sense of their ADHD diagnosis. And these concepts aren't linear: they intersect organically backward and forward.

- How do I **recognize** my ADHD symptoms?
- How do I **accept** my ADHD?
- How do I continue to **educate** myself about ADHD to better understand myself?
- How do I continue to **integrate** ADHD into my life every day?

These powerful concepts become a framework for living successfully with ADHD.

Recognition

As a first step, you have to recognize that you have symptoms of ADHD, whether you have an official diagnosis or not. These symptoms might include difficulties prioritizing your to-do list, trouble focusing on the task at hand, and feeling like your emotions have a mind of their own.[4] I'm not telling you whether or not to seek an official diagnosis, though a certain sense of relief may come with receiving one. But once ADHD is recognized, many people find that behaviors from the past suddenly make more sense.

> *Okay, that's why I would walk from my bedroom to the laundry room and do five tasks en route but forget what I went to do in the first place.*
>
> *Ah-ha, that explains why I blurt things out and don't let people finish their sentences. I get excited and can't seem to stop myself from jumping in. . . .*

You are the only one who can determine if getting a diagnosis from a medical or clinical professional is needed for you to recognize your neurodiversity. You can also take an online assessment as a first step in this journey.[5]

Acceptance

You may need some time to accept your ADHD diagnosis and make peace with it. Some of my clients are anxious they'll use their diagnosis as an excuse or scapegoat for certain challenging behaviors. For instance, one client was worried she'd start to blame her ADHD for being late and that felt like a cop-out to her. I asked her: "If you were diagnosed with hearing loss, and needed to wear a hearing aid, would you see that as 'making excuses'?" Hopefully, you'll see ADHD as a form of neurodiversity that requires scaffolding to reduce the disruptive impacts on your life and to emphasize its positive elements too.

In the case of my client worried about using ADHD as an excuse for frequently being late, we unpacked that together. We discussed the actions she could take now that she had this awareness. She bought old-fashioned, loud alarm clocks for different rooms of her house and her desk. She also built buffers into her calendar around meetings. Acceptance of how her ADHD manifested helped her develop the right tactics to address it.

Part of accepting your ADHD is also getting comfortable with the idea that you will need support. Ideally, your family and friends are supportive. And connecting with an association like TotallyADD or Children and Adults with Attention-Deficit/ Hyperactivity Disorder (CHADD) may provide valuable connections to others who are learning how to manage their ADHD diagnoses. Many companies have affinity groups to support neurodiverse staff in the workplace. Taking advantage of support groups is a powerful way to build your acceptance of your ADHD.

You have ADHD. There is nothing to be ashamed about. You are neurodiverse. Congratulations! I hope you realize there is much to celebrate about this diagnosis, such as the ability to juggle many issues at once, the ability to generate a lot of energy that inspires others, and the ability to tap into creative superpowers.

It's hard to argue with the success of folks such as Olympic gold medalists Michael Phelps and Simone Biles, entrepreneur Richard Branson (who also has dyslexia), and celebrities like Justin Timberlake and Emma Watson: they all famously celebrate their ADHD as a superpower. And let's not forget historical notables such as Mozart, Einstein, da Vinci, Alexander Graham Bell, and Eleanor Roosevelt who all supposedly had ADHD.[6]

I am loud and proud of my neurodiversity. And I hope you will be too. Every day, I strive to improve my performance and my way of interacting with others. We are all works in progress and self-acceptance is a critical step.

Recognition and Acceptance – My Story Sometimes a child receives an ADHD diagnosis, as my son did, and the parent thinks "Hey, that sounds like me!" That was my situation exactly.

I saw myself so clearly, really for the first time, when I started probing how my son's diagnosis mirrored my own behaviors and frustrations. I remembered feeling as a child that too much was going on in my head. I couldn't organize my thoughts and felt out of control. Growing up, teachers had always commented on my outbursts in the classroom.

I found workarounds to these tendencies as I grew older, but I always thought it was my fault and simply a question of self-control. My internal narrative was "It's my problem and I have to fix it with more self-discipline."

- I was infamous at work for interrupting others during meetings. I didn't know how to control my enthusiasm and also was afraid I'd miss my chance to share my comment if I didn't jump in as soon as the thought entered my head.
- Numerous people reporting to me over the years shared their frustrations with how I delegated. I often moved too fast and didn't fully brief them on the context and expectations of a project. That translated into them not feeling set up for success.

After receiving my adult ADHD diagnosis, I found it challenging at first to apply the label to myself. "Do I feel comfortable referring to myself as neurodiverse?" But much more important was the profound relief I started to feel once I recognized and accepted I had ADHD.

Oh, I'm not just a distractible person. There are reasons why I say and do things impulsively beyond not having self-control.

Ironically, my diagnosis felt like I regained some control over my life and helped me develop enormous empathy for my clients who struggle with ADHD symptoms. For instance, I helped one client get to the point where she was comfortable sharing her diagnosis with her boss. She then spearheaded the neurodiversity affinity group at her company. That was the result of her accepting and integrating her ADHD diagnosis into her role as an executive, and recognizing there was no shame in it. She had to reframe her personal narrative to incorporate ADHD before she could positively impact others.

Education

Many folks get a diagnosis of ADHD and start frantically searching the internet. The good news is that there are tons of resources out there. That is also the bad news because it's easy to do a deep dive and get overwhelmed. Start slowly with one site, such as Additudemag.com. Numerous podcasts also are up and running, including *I Have ADHD* and *Faster Than Normal*. Pick one or two whose style appeals to you. It's a marathon not a sprint. In Appendix 2, I share a curated list of excellent ADHD resources, many of which are referenced in this chapter.

You probably got your diagnosis from a psychologist or maybe you completed an online assessment and have a self-diagnosis. If you are considering medication, consult with a medical professional since they are the only ones who can prescribe meds. The first step is to educate yourself about the pros and cons of medication. Also remember, you can decide on one path today and change your mind down the road. I have clients who were on medication for years who stopped because they didn't feel they needed it any longer. I have others who were anti-medication but found out later that they benefited from it.

For myself, I worked with a psychiatrist to determine if I needed medication. After experimentation under his guidance, I currently only take medication when I'm involved in a particularly challenging and overwhelming project like learning new software, doing my taxes, or writing a book! That may change as my life evolves, and my psychiatrist and I connect quarterly to monitor the situation.

Meditation was the biggest game changer for me and is an ever-evolving journey. I started with transcendental meditation, lapsed, read some books, and tried again. Along the way I joined two different meditation groups, and even completed a 10-day silent meditation—one of the most challenging experiences of my life. My current daily practice is 20 minutes in the morning, and right now I am using the 10 Percent Happier app. Meditation grounds me. I can now create more of a pause between thinking, feeling, and acting.

Today, ADHD coaching services are available both in real life and online, making them more accessible. In the past few years, the number of online programs and apps focused on supporting folks with ADHD diagnoses has also exploded, and they come with different price tags and the list keeps growing. Read user reviews and take advantage of free trials to get a sense of fit for you. Be a discerning consumer.

Educating yourself about ADHD doesn't stop. The research keeps expanding and the available online and offline tools keep multiplying. Continue to approach ADHD with a learning mindset to feel more in control of your condition and your options.

Do I Need an ADHD Coach or an Executive Coach? If you are thinking about engaging a coach, explore whether an ADHD coach or an executive coach who has experience with ADHD is the best fit. They are different specialties.

I am an executive coach who has some clients with ADHD, which is different from being an ADHD coach. I coach experienced executives and up-and-coming leaders; in some cases, they have ADHD diagnoses; in others, they have many of the symptoms but have not received an official diagnosis. I incorporate ADHD into the coaching journey with these clients, rather than it being the primary focus of the coaching.

I deeply empathize and resonate with my clients' ADHD journeys to deal with their symptoms and frustrations. I overlay my knowledge of ADHD, experience living with it, and coaching others with it on to our coaching work.

Some folks may want to work with an ADHD coach because they have significant challenges maintaining attention and focus, organizing and prioritizing, and handling emotional regulation. An ADHD coach often focuses on accountability: the coach will help you get organized, plan and prioritize, and develop systems to improve your focus.[7]

ADHD Coaching Challenge

For someone with ADHD, ask yourself these questions as you consider what kind of coaching will best meet your needs.

- Are my ADHD symptoms (e.g., lack of focus and ability to prioritize) impeding me from (at least) adequately performing at work?
- Are my ADHD symptoms getting in the way of me having (at least) adequate relations with my co-workers, direct reports, and managers?
- Am I unable to adequately self-regulate my emotions on the job and in the rest of life?

If you answer yes to two or all three of these questions, my suggestion is to investigate working with an ADHD coach first. That will give you a tactical, practical base from which to launch your journey with an executive coach.

Integration

Integrating ADHD into your life is a personal journey about self-knowledge, and there is no one way to be successful. Everyone has to find their own path. The key is knowing that there is a path out there for you.

- How do you integrate neurodiversity into your self-narrative?
- How much do you want to share with the world about your ADHD?
- How open are you to asking for and accepting help?
- How do you befriend your ADHD so you can live together in relative peace?

How you answer these questions will inform your integration path. I have clients who decided not to share their ADHD with colleagues, while others were so relieved to realize they had a neurodiverse condition to help understand their behavior that they wanted to shout the news from the rooftops. In my experience, clients often don't share much with others about their ADHD until they have had time to absorb the news. How long that takes differs from person to person.

Integration – My Story

I already had organizational and productivity systems in place that I had built up through my years as a student and in my professional life. I was high-functioning, regardless of my ADHD, but I knew I needed more help to achieve my potential and to show up for others the way I wanted to—focused, calm, patient, and present. I was able to offer that help to myself, through what I had learned and practiced as an executive coach. A great deal of the journey was about reframing how I saw myself, building new awareness of my strengths and challenges, and using my coaching frameworks and recipes as additional scaffolding in my work and personal life.

For example, I have used the COIN framework (Chapter 9) to help me prepare for and have tough conversations more times than I can count. I leaned on this framework recently to discuss missed deadlines by my graphic designer that resulted in a delayed client proposal. The framework helped me to control my emotions and stay on point, and end interactions on a productive note.

Today, I speak openly about my ADHD. I'm at ease with it. I integrate my ADHD into how I present myself to the world. It has unexpectedly become part of my brand! For instance, recently, I was at a conference and said to someone I had just met:

> *This room is so crowded, and I have an adult diagnosis of ADHD, and that gets in the way of me focusing on you. Can we move to a quieter corner to continue our conversation?*
>
> *The guy suggested we grab a couple of chairs on the other side of the room where we could hear better.*

I felt centered and genuine. I recognized how deeply I had integrated ADHD into my self-perception—the superpowers, the challenges, and the commitment to working with it, instead of struggling against it.

This book can support you on the journey of recognizing and accepting your ADHD, educating yourself about it, and integrating it into your life. Let's get started!

Reflection Questions

- Do I need a coach to help me through this?
- Do I need medication?
- How much do I want to share about my ADHD—personally and professionally?
- What is my next step on this journey of self-knowledge?

Resources

See Appendix 2 for a curated list of ADHD resources, including books, websites, podcasts, and more.

4

How to Use the Rest of the Book

I wrote this book because I want to give you coaching tools that will help when you need support at work and/or in the rest of your life. In Parts II, III, and IV, I share my "go-to" coaching frameworks. These are the heart of the book. They are the frameworks I have found to have the most universal relevance, and the ones I have relied on in my coaching practice time and time again to generate powerful results. And they can be of service to you in myriad ways in myriad circumstances.

Here is how I suggest you navigate Parts II, III, and IV.

You don't have to read the sections in order. Having said that, you can't go wrong by starting with Part II since examining your values, and knowing the frameworks I use to launch coaching engagements, is a good starting place. After that, you can move right to management tools (Part IV), even if you aren't a manager, or you can look at the communication frameworks if you have a challenging conversation coming up or a relationship glitch to navigate (Part III). Each part of the book includes three or four different frameworks.

At the back of the book, in Appendix 1, you'll find an easy reference guide to all 11 of the coaching frameworks.

Lean on the frameworks as you begin your self-discovery journey. I follow coaching frameworks more closely if elements of the coaching engagement are unfamiliar to me. Just like when I'm following a recipe for the first time, I follow it very closely. When I have made the same cake recipe a few times, then I'll start experimenting with ingredients and technique variations. I use the same logic with coaching frameworks.

How you use a framework will depend on your experience, confidence, and the situation. For instance, if you have never negotiated your salary before, I'd expect you to rely more heavily on the COIN framework (Part III), but even the most experienced negotiator can benefit from reminders about communication tactics by reviewing this framework.

A framework is essentially a support structure that exists to make it easier for you to do something, similar to a recipe. I use *framework* and *recipe* interchangeably in this book. A tactic is different. I think of tactics as hacks that you apply in the moment.

I know the frameworks in this book are relevant for anyone who is curious and has a passion for personal learning and professional development. Obviously, for someone with ADHD, implementing the frameworks may include some additional considerations, and I point those out along the way. I also share case studies of my clients with ADHD throughout the book to hone in on some of the different strategies they employ.

Part V is about how to get your coaching wins to stick. That is: How do you keep up the awareness you have developed and continue to utilize the new behaviors that have brought you success? To be honest, this is the hardest part of coaching . . . and the most rewarding. When you see yourself navigate new situations, drawing upon a larger toolkit of frameworks, strategies and tactics, it is immensely rewarding.

I leave the conversation about habits and other strategies to solidify coaching wins until after you have gone through the frameworks, and ideally, utilized some of them to enact change.

But if you think there is information here that will help you before diving into the frameworks, then feel free to start with Part V.

A final logistical note before we dive in. When you coach yourself, pen and paper (even better, a substantial notebook and pen you love to use) are your best friends. Yes, I am suggesting that you don't use your phone or laptop to answer the reflection questions and exercise prompts scattered throughout the book. Research shows that pen and paper is more effective than your laptop when taking notes because you retain more and are less prone to distraction.[1]

Onward! I'm excited to lead you through my "go-to" frameworks. I am confident you'll increase your awareness and change behaviors. Be prepared to be patient, to practice, and to positively reinforce yourself along the way. Change is tough, but have fun with this. Challenge yourself and think about how good it will feel as you learn more about yourself and put that into action in how you interact with others—both at work and in the rest of life.

II

Coaching Frameworks
for Takeoff

Starting a coaching journey has three key aspects. Chapter 5 covers understanding your values and how they serve as your starting point. Chapter 6 introduces a simple, flexible framework to help define your coaching goals. Finally, how you view your role vis-à-vis the challenge you are tackling is the focus of Chapter 7.

5

Core Values Framework: Anchor Your Journey

Knowing yourself is the beginning of all wisdom.

—Aristotle

Defining Your Values Is the First Step

Values are our North Star. Your core values are the principles or standards of behavior that are formed by life experiences and codes of conduct, implicitly and explicitly, from our family, culture, religion, life experiences, and own inner work. When we remember them, they keep us honest and focused. They anchor us to what matters because people are happiest when what they are doing on the outside is congruent with their values on the inside.

- **What is important to me now?**
- **How do my values inform my purpose?**
- **How am I incorporating these values through my work and my relationships?**

Defining our values helps us prioritize our goals. I launch *every* coaching engagement with a values exercise. It's a reminder of what's important to you and where we are starting. If you are contemplating career transition, it is a critical first step in coaching. How can you decide about your next career move if you aren't clear about your values? Values help us define our priorities.

For instance, Jenny was a client who had rowed crew in college, and that sense of camaraderie stayed with her. When she did this values exercise, it helped guide her as she looked for her next role. She wanted to work closely with others, and not work for long stretches alone. She was ultimately in the fortunate position of having two job opportunities to choose between, and she chose the one in the earlier-stage company where the founder emphasized teamwork and she would be working on multiple cross-functional teams.

Is teamwork a value? I don't get hung up on strict definitions of what is or isn't a value. What matters is that your values should help prioritize and guide you in how you live your life.

Launching a coaching engagement, most clients can't name their values. I want my clients to have their values on the tip of their tongue and to work them into their daily conversations and recall them when they confront challenging situations. We work to identify values by answering questions such as:

- **When was the last time that you thought deeply about how to articulate your values?**
- **Can you name your core values easily?**
- **Do you feel like your values guide your day-to-day actions? If so, how?**

Values can change over time. It makes sense that your 25-year-old self valued adventure more than stability. That's why we need to check in on our values and see if they have evolved, particularly in the vicinity of a major transition.

- **Which changes over the past few years have impacted your values? (e.g., work, relationships, family)?**
- **Have you experienced a shift in your values over time?**
- **What can you learn about your purpose from understanding these value shifts?**

My Values   When I launched my coaching business, one of the first things I did was create a values exercise and complete it myself. And my core values have remained constant since then. Here are my five values, and I created a mnemonic to recall them easily (GLIPP).

- Gratitude
- Learning mindset/curiosity
- In service of potential
- Productivity
- Positivity

In my 20s, I would never have considered gratitude an important value. It is now core to how I show up every day—including having a gratitude journaling practice. I have definitely shifted from being hungry to experience more and more to a place where I am grateful for everything in my life.

I try to remember to use my values in my daily language. I also check proposals to ensure I include them when possible. And when I'm asked to answer that "tell me what you do" question, I always reply with some variation of "I work in the service of helping others develop their potential."

Core Values Exercise

I have my clients do this exercise on their own, and we discuss their results during one of our first meetings. We then refer to their values throughout our work together.

I recommend that you sit somewhere quiet and dedicate some time to this exercise. And ideally revisit your results a couple of days later to see if you'd refine your list.

Step 1. Brainstorm Your Long List of Values

Reflect on your values without referring to any list. This might be easy or challenging for you, but starting with a list of several dozen values can be overwhelming. As my client Lipi said, "All the values looked good to me, I had a hard time choosing! I found it easier to think about my values with a blank piece of paper in front of me before consulting the list."

Once you have made a first attempt at identifying your values, you can refer to a list of values for inspiration and more nuance. There are literally hundreds of possible values, as you can see from my abbreviated list that follows. Brene Brown's website[1] also offers a lengthy list of values to consult. Your initial values list might be quite long, and that's totally fine.

Core Values

Accomplishment	Bravery	Composure
Adaptability	Calmness	Confidence
Ambition	Candor	Connection
Appreciation	Challenge	Courage
Awe	Commitment	Curiosity
Balance	Compassion	Diplomacy
Boldness	Competition	Efficiency

Empathy	Independence	Reliability
Endurance	Insightfulness	Resilience
Energy	Integrity	Resourcefulness
Faith	Intimacy	Respect
Fame	Joy	Rigor
Fearlessness	Justice	Sacredness
Flow	Kindness	Security
Focus	Knowledge	Service
Fun	Leadership	Silence
Generosity	Learning	Spontaneity
Grace	Logic	Stability
Gratitude	Love	Strength
Happiness	Loyalty	Success
Hard Work	Mastery	Support
Harmony	Mindfulness	Synergy
Health	Motivation	Teamwork
Heart	Open-mindedness	Tenacity
Helpfulness	Optimism	Trust
Honesty	Originality	Truth
Honor	Peacefulness	Uniqueness
Hopefulness	Perfection	Unity
Humility	Playfulness	Vision
Humor	Practicality	Wisdom
Impact	Proactivity	Wonder

Step 2. Choose Your Top 10 Values

Select your top 10 values from the longer list you initially brainstormed and write them down. If you don't see a value that speaks to you on a list, create your own. See if you can combine any of them since values may overlap.

Step 3. Finalize Your Core Values

Finalize a list of five core values from your top 10 list, ideally in priority order. These questions will help to finalize your list of five core values.

- **Which values are core to you living your life?**
- **When these values aren't present in an experience or relationship, do you feel uncomfortable? When they are being honored, do you feel aligned?**
- **Do these values help you make decisions?**

My client Carlos, a start-up founder, came up with a list of 10 values, we combined them where there was overlap and ended up with a list of five that really spoke to him.

- Carlos's first cut of top 10 values: accomplishment, challenge, control, freedom, learning, humility, justice, structure, growth, determination.
- Carlos's five core values narrowed down from his top 10 values: challenge, freedom, structure, learning, determination.

Step 4. Activate Your Core Values

Now that you have a list of five core values, define what each value means for you in your daily life, and when you grapple with larger challenges and opportunities. In Carlos's case, this is where he ended up:

- Challenge: I seek out opportunities that push me to be my best.
- Freedom: I have the ability to pursue my ideas without constraints placed on me by others.
- Structure: I build what's important to me and can be scaled.

- Learning: I am in an environment of constant learning or I get bored and distracted.
- Determination: When I have a goal to pursue, I don't give up.

During our work together, Carlos faced numerous challenges around his company's growth, and he leaned into his values to help keep him honest about what he was good at and what the company needed. After several months, he realized that he needed to bring in someone to manage operations so the company could scale more easily. In his words:

I knew what my values were but activating them was more challenging. I didn't want to give up on my goal of building my business but I also wanted to activate my core values of freedom and structure, so I needed to bring in someone else to help to grow operations in a healthy way.

Key Reminders as You Think about Your Core Values

- Some clients ask me. "Am I defining my work and life values or just my work values?" My answer is always to answer as a whole person since that is what you are; there isn't a "work" you and a "rest of the life" you, is there?
- Others ask me: "Can't I pick more than five values?" Of course you can. But it's much easier to have a short list that truly reflects your priorities in life. The short list takes more effort and discipline.
- When you have completed this exercise, put these values somewhere prominent. I put them on a sticky on the wall near my desk. I also put them on the first page of my journal.
- I also encourage my clients to verbalize their values in the day-to-day. And this is a helpful tactic in work interviews and performance reviews. For instance,

- "I want to thank you for giving me that feedback, having a learning mindset is one of my key values."
- "I am happy to make that introduction, being a connector is one of my key values."
- "I'm glad that my boss recognized my contributions as a strong team member in my performance review because teamwork is one of my core values."

Adrianne and Her Job Search   My client Adrianne had been COO of an early-stage data services company for several years. She had decided it was time to move on. After the refinement process, these were her top values, and we activated them to identify what she wanted from her next career move.

Adrianne's Values Mapped to Her Job Search

Accomplishment	I want to build a great company and see it grow.
Curiosity	I want to work on something interesting that I'll be excited to learn about and think about all the time.
Freedom	I want to be in charge! I am ready to start my own company.
Adventure	I prioritize working at a company where international travel is part of my role.
Empathy	I want to build an organizational culture where people bring their whole selves to work, and feel respected and able to express themselves fully.

Adrianne articulated that this values exercise helped her realize that she was ready to start her own company. That was a real revelation. "This exercise was so helpful. It helped set me on my path with a lot more clarity." Adrianne spent several months identifying the right incubator and the strongest business idea to develop. As I finish this book, Adrianne has successfully launched a successful online mental health app, and has fundraised for the company's next stage of growth.

Reflection Questions

- How are my core values showing up in my everyday life?
- How am I using my values to anchor my decision making at work and in my relationships?
- How do my values provide context and guidance for me as I think about next steps, for instance, with my career?

Resources

- *The Practice of Adaptive Leadership: Tools and Tactics for Changing Your Organization and the World* by Ronald A. Heifetz, Marty Linsky, and Alexander Grashow, Harvard Business Review Press (2009). This is a guide to approaching leadership in a rapidly changing world, including a deep dive into values and power.
- *Dare to Lead* by Brene Brown, Ebury Publishing (2018). I have this book on my Kindle, on my bookshelf, and as an audio book. It has powerful leadership insights, and practical tools to activate leadership best practices in your daily life. And Brene Brown always anchors her work in values.
- *The Power of Purpose* by Richard Leider, Berrett-Koehler Publishers (2010). This book emphasizes putting your values into action to live a life of purpose. It offers tools for unlocking your own purpose.

6

Mind the Gap Framework

Without a gap, there is no coaching.

—Fred Kofman

Have you used the Tube (subway) in London? If so, you have heard the recording over the loudspeaker in some tube stations "Mind the Gap." This announcement is played when a train is in the station and there is a gap between the platform and the train. I love this image because it depicts the start of the coaching journey so well. You are on the platform (starting point) and you want to get on the train (destination). What lies between these two points is the gap—the liminal space. This is where we do our coaching work.

Understanding the Mind the Gap Framework

Hands down, this Mind the Gap framework (Figure 6.1) is at the heart of my coaching process. I might argue that you can't have a coaching engagement without this framework. It is what everything hangs on.

Figure 6.1 Mind the Gap Framework.

The essence of coaching for me starts by helping my client define their current state and the future state they want to achieve. Our coaching work takes place in the gap between those two states. Here's how you can apply this framework in your own life with or without a coach.

Define Your Current State

- **How would you describe your situation today?**
- **How would you describe your challenge?**

By situation, I mean your external context and your current thoughts and behaviors. People usually engage a coach because there is a challenge they are trying to overcome. This is the starting point. Sometimes clients need time to develop this awareness but defining key challenges is usually the easiest part of the coaching process—and the most important.

For example, after two coaching sessions, my client Sarah, an attorney at a large law firm, defined her current state as follows:

I lack the confidence to share my opinions in a persuasive way, and in person is harder for me than in writing, and I believe this is getting in the way of a promotion.

As Sarah told me, "I am afraid of saying the wrong thing in meetings. The stakes seem too high to get it wrong. I worry that if

I say the wrong thing it will affect how the partners view me and my abilities, and ultimately will affect my ability to get promoted."

Define Your Future State

I encourage clients to capture this vision of the future in a detailed way with words and to think of it as a snapshot of future success.

- **What is your vision of what change looks like for you?**
- **What will you be doing differently?**
- **How can you visualize this change with all of your senses?**

Continuing Sarah's example, she defined her future state this way:

I see myself sitting in meetings with my peers, and more senior attorneys and partners confidently and fluently sharing my opinions with a clear voice and a calm delivery. I will no longer be second guessing myself so much.

An important distinction exists between defining the future state that you want to achieve and the outcome that you are working toward. Sarah clarified for herself that the future state she was focused on was sharing her opinions, and that those opinions would be respected and considered. That in itself is different from wanting the outcome to be a promotion. Sarah was focused on demonstrating behaviors that she believed would open doorways for her, including promotion.

Mind the Gap

The space where I spend most of my time with coaching clients is the gap between the current and future state.

- **What is going on in the gap that gets in the way of the future state that you want to create for yourself?**

This liminal space can be vast and includes personal awareness, perceptions of others, skills, resources, relationships, systems, organizational dynamics, and more—the list is extensive and unique to each person.

The coaching work in the gap is threefold:

- Prioritize the changes to be made and attach them to specific goals linked to the future vision.
- Prioritize what is in the gap that is most important to achieving these goals and the future vision.
- Create an action plan in which priority issues in the gap are turned into step goals and related specific actions.

In Sarah's case, in the gap, we prioritized exploring how her background and messages she had internalized about authority and risk taking were holding her back.

Questions Sarah and I explored included:

- **Did you ever feel confident expressing yourself in groups? If so, what were the specific circumstances?**
- **How do you feel about taking risks? How can you explore making risk taking more accessible?**
- **What is your relationship with authority and how has that helped you in the past, and how might it be getting in the way of your future vision?**

As Sarah developed more awareness about some of her attitudes and self-beliefs, she began to see that other options were available to her. We created a goal around how to prepare herself for critical meetings and monitor her participation during these meetings. This included:

- Reading all the documents and preparing some questions or talking points at least six hours before a meeting (so she had time to reach out to others, if she had clarification questions).

- Writing out notes about the meeting attendees and their styles, so she could have this front of mind during the meeting (for instance, she knew some partners like very detailed answers, while others just want the answer but want to know you have the information to back it up, if needed).

- Holding five minutes on her calendar before meetings to repeat her mantra "You've got this, Sarah" and to practice a deep-breathing exercise she had honed and found helped lower her anxiety.

- Finally, during those five minutes, she visualized herself acting in the way she wanted to be known for—calm, confident, and in command of the material.

And we created an accountability system to monitor her success in achieving this goal by having a trusted colleague give her feedback on her meeting presence and participation.

Another goal was to tap into the senior network of women at her firm for mentoring. A final goal was to take a public speaking course. We also did significant role playing inside our coaching sessions where she practiced using her voice and influencing skills and I challenged her on them.

How to Use This Framework without a Coach

- As mentioned, I launch my coaching engagements with this framework. When you use it yourself, think of it as a diagnostic tool. When you have a challenge to work through, move away from your laptop and find some time with pen and paper. The reflections are more profound.[1]

- You may need to go through the Mind the Gap exercise a few times before you get to the essence of what is in your gap, and steps you can take to close the gap to arrive at your desired future state.

- Do you have trusted colleagues, friends, or family who could help you work through the framework? Another person's perspective can be helpful.

Reflection Questions

- Current State: What isn't working today for me? How would I describe my current state if I was an observer of myself, my situation, and my behaviors?
- Future State: What is my vision for how I want things to be for me in the future? How can I describe that future state with as much sensory detail as possible? Can I also describe the future state in terms of behaviors that I want to see myself exhibit?
- The Gap: What is getting in my way of achieving my vision? Are there self-beliefs? Perceptions of others? Specific behaviors? If I don't feel I have all the answers now, how can I seek out more information about what is in the gap?

Resources

- *Coaching Skills: The Definitive Guide to Being a Coach, Fourth Edition* by Jenny Rogers, McGraw-Hill Education (2016). This was my bible when I took my executive coaching course at NYU. Jenny Rogers covers all aspects of coaching in this book, and the chapter on launching an engagement is particularly good. This book is aimed at the practitioner.
- *The Coaching Manual: The Definitive Guide to The Process, Principles and Skills of Personal Coaching, Fourth Edition* by Julie Starr, Pearson Education (2021). Another comprehensive book that walks you through all aspects of coaching, including launching an engagement. It's also aimed at the practitioner.

7

Spectator-Actor Mindset Framework

We don't get to choose what happens to us, but we do get to choose how we respond to our experience.

—Edith Eger

We all find ourselves in situations where we feel like we have no control and all we can do is react to what is happening to us. We don't feel powerful in such instances; we often feel powerless. I challenge you to think about the options open to you when you confront super challenging situations. Lead with this mindset when you start to unravel a challenge that you want to coach yourself on.

Understanding the Spectator-Actor Mindset Framework

This framework helps you analyze a challenge facing you with an actor mindset (What can I control? What are my options?) instead of a spectator mindset (What is happening to me? Who is doing this to me?). While it's logical to start from a spectator perspective and try to understand what is happening to you, if you get stuck there, you miss the opportunity to explore options and to feel more in control.

I'm not saying this mindset will ensure the successful outcome you want; however, it allows you to tap into your values (see Chapter 5), and consider a path forward aligned with your values. And ultimately, isn't that real success?

Which Mindset Is Going to Serve You Best?

Spectator Mindset	Actor Mindset
You feel defensiveness and experience a lack of choices.	You feel responsible.
When things aren't going your way, it's tempting to feel like things are being done to you, and you are powerless to change the situation.	You always have the ability to decide how you respond to a situation, while acknowledging that you can face external factors beyond your control.
Focuses on: • What happened to me. • Factors I can't influence. • External circumstances I am at the mercy of. • Lack acknowledgment of own contribution to the current situation. • When things go wrong, resorts to blame.	Focuses on: • What my responsibility is in this situation. • What I can influence. • How to do my personal best and build my self-esteem. • Recognition that reality isn't wrong, what changes is how I deal with it. • When I act in alignment with my values, I am more successful, even if the outcome is different from the one I desire.

Use This Framework All the Time

I use this framework all the time in my coaching practice. I find it helpful at the beginning of an engagement to help define the major coaching goal. I want my client to unpack his perceptions of the situation he is confronting. I want him to acknowledge that he always has options, even if it doesn't initially feel that way. This unpacking helps ensure our coaching goals are on target.

For a client deciding how to handle an unreasonable boss, I spend time with him asking questions grounded in this framework. For instance:

- **How would your boss explain this situation?**
- **What is your responsibility in creating this situation?**
- **What options are open to you to understand and potentially act in this situation?**
- **What can you do differently?**
- **What did you learn?**

I also refer to this framework during a coaching engagement if I feel my client is slipping into a mindset of "why is this being done to me?" The beauty of this framework is that you also can apply it on a daily basis to evaluate your mindset. It's about shifting your mindset.

For something simple like a reaction you have to a colleague who ignored you in a meeting, it might be enough to ask yourself:

- **What was going on? What was I perceiving?**
- **What responsibility did I have in that situation?**
- **Can I think of something different that I could have done in the meeting or ways that I could have prepared better?**

Tips for Using This Framework Yourself

- Start with determining what is purely external, what is within your control, and then delve into how you can respond as an actor rather than a spectator in your drama.

- This framework helps you generate options. It is a fantastic tool for exploring paths forward.
- This framework assumes that you are open minded to responding differently and you believe in your ability to respond differently to achieve the future state you desire.
- Bear in mind that new responses (focus on being an actor) do not guarantee new outcomes. The focus is on acting in line with your integrity and growing toward your goals.

Daria's Dilemma: Stay or Move On The Spectator-Actor Mindset framework is helpful if you are deciding whether to work through a challenging work situation or move on. My client Daria was brought in by the founder of a prestigious management consulting firm to head up a new practice area for nonprofit organizations. She was a deeply experienced consultant and leader in the nonprofit sector. One of her peers at the new firm was a highly regarded technology practice lead who generated a lot of business for the firm. He made her life difficult from the beginning. He didn't support building the nonprofit practice area because he thought it would hurt the firm's overall profitability, and he didn't like her style, which he perceived as not bottom-line focused enough. He didn't tell her directly: she heard about his issues with her from others. After almost a year at the firm, Daria came to me because she was stressed navigating this situation alone. She had tried to get support from the firm's CEO but found him unresponsive.

Daria and I worked together for several months. At first, Daria expressed herself as someone who was trapped. In her view, the problem was her colleague's behavior and she felt stuck without any viable options for change—except to leave. The stress affected her confidence in her own abilities and others noticed it, too.

Over time, Daria began to see her role in the situation differently, and took more responsibility for her actions. We worked on an action plan that included strategies, criteria to measure progress, and a timeline.

- She worked on tactics to call out her colleague if he undermined her in meetings.
- She sought out inputs from other colleagues before key meetings, so she could speak from a place of "we" not "I."
- She did a listening tour with key stakeholders about the new practice area's strategy, budget, and her leadership of the team. She embraced the stakeholder feedback and integrated it into her strategy and style.
- She also consulted with the firm's CEO and concluded he was not going to hold her colleague accountable. She was clear that she'd have to shift the dynamics of the situation herself or leave.

Once she'd decided to shift into the mindset of an actor, she dedicated six months to see if meaningful change was possible or she'd move on.

Daria reported feeling more empowered and having more agency during those six months. She felt more confident as she implemented her action steps. She saw some improvements in her colleague's interactions with her as well. At the end of the six months, she hadn't decided whether to leave. But after another three months, she decided to join another consulting firm, where the culture felt more aligned with her values.

Daria proved that she was capable of new responses, but that did not guarantee new outcomes. Through our coaching work Daria realized that acting with integrity and in line with her own growth goals was the measure of real success. This required evaluating the situation from a position of agency to determine whether the situation could be meaningfully changed for the better and whether this firm was a good fit for her. Ultimately she decided it wasn't and she moved on.

Carolina's Dilemma: Business School or New Job   This framework also can help you revisit your options from a perspective of agency when you need to evaluate opportunities. A young executive I mentored, Carolina, was deciding between multiple job offers from start-ups or whether to go to business school. Through coaching, she determined that going to business school was her first choice. At the same time, Carolina believed she had to abide by the companies' decision deadlines and accept or reject the job offers before knowing if she was accepted at her first choice for business school. She struggled not to close doors with potential employers if she didn't get accepted into her top business school choice. We were meeting on Saturday and the job offers had Monday deadlines and business school acceptance letters would arrive on Wednesday or Thursday. She felt at the mercy of these externalities. She felt trapped.

I asked her to compare how someone with a spectator mindset or an actor mindset would respond in this situation. We talked it through using this framework as our anchor. She decided to call the business school first thing Monday morning and ask them for an early indication so she could factor that into her decision about the job offers.

Her first-choice business school shared that she was accepted and she was going to receive a scholarship! Carolina was fortunate the business school was flexible. But even if they had said she had to wait, she had prepared her talking points for the various employers. She planned to tell them she couldn't answer until later in the week, and if that meant she was out of the running, she was prepared to live with that outcome. She was prepared to act, not simply spectate. The key here is that she did not have control over the situation, but she had agency over how she responded. Not only did she get into business school with a scholarship, but also one of the firms she turned down for full time work hired her as a summer intern.

Reflection Questions

- Are there any situations you currently face where you feel like things are happening TO you? Are you using phrases to describe the situation such as "the problem is . . . ," "I have done my best but . . . ," "I can't believe I'm being treated this way . . ."
- Ask yourself: What can I do differently? How am I challenged? Am I willing to try something else to reach my goal (desired future state)?
- How can you stay curious? Can you use open-ended questions to really get to the root problem that you need to solve for?
- What are my options as an actor in this drama? How can I avoid seeing myself as a spectator without power and options?
- Am I acting aligned with my values?

Resources

- *Conscious Business* by Fred Kofman, ReadHowYouWant.com, Ltd. (2002). I was lucky enough to take a course with Fred, by far the best coaching course I have taken to date. His emphasis on role playing as part of the coaching process was a game changer for me.
- *The Gift: 12 Lessons to Save Your Life* by Edith Eger (2020). She survived a concentration camp during WWII. This book offers many highly actionable tactics to put her life lessons into forward motion in your life. My favorite exercise

was analyzing my self-talk for a day and determining what empowered me and what depleted me.

- *Man's Search for Meaning* by Victor Frankel (1946). You've likely heard of this classic, but have you taken the time to read it? A concentration camp survivor whose writing is a true gift for anyone interested in better understanding resilience, the power of the mind, and the value of hope.

Navigating Challenging Conversations

This is the most important part of the book because life is one long journey of communicating! Regardless of the reason a client comes to me for coaching, communication strategies and tactics usually become a focus area of at least some of our work together. I frequently help clients communicate more effectively when they need to have a challenging conversation with a boss, colleague, or team member. These frameworks work equally well in your personal life, too.

The framework you choose will depend on the particular situation you face. And the four building blocks covered in Chapter 8 will help you utilize these frameworks more efficiently. From there we move on to:

- **COIN** (Common Purpose, Observations, Inquiry, Next Steps) (Chapter 9) is my go-to checklist for any conversation that causes discomfort.
- **Communicate FOR** framework (Chapter 10) is most helpful when the relationship is more important than immediate conflict resolution.

- **Compassionate Candor** (Chapter 11) is my go-to framework for delivering effective feedback.
- The **Conversation Funnel** (Chapter 12) will help you better prepare for and engage in an important conversation or meeting.

How do we define a challenging conversation

One that makes you feel vulnerable, and your self-esteem or skills are being questioned. Or it could be a conversation you believe will upset someone else where the stakes are high and the outcome uncertain. Examples include:

- Calling your parents to tell them you are dropping out of law school.
- Informing your boss you are leaving after she promoted you last month.
- Telling a team member her displays of anger are affecting her ability to be promoted.

Conversations we dread are often conversations we postpone. And as the cycle of dread and postponement continues, our stress rises, the situation often gets worse, and resolution is even more unlikely. If you develop the skills to have such conversations, you will have less anxiety, more confidence in your communication skills, and a stronger sense of integrity.

8

Four Key Building Blocks
for Critical Conversations

People will forget what you said, people will forget what you did, but people never forget how you made them feel.

—Maya Angelou

As you prepare for a challenging conversation, assemble these four key building blocks: preparation, curiosity, active listening, and the ability to ask open-ended questions to set yourself up for success.

Preparation

If you take one tip away from reading this book, it is this: always prepare for critical conversations. They invariably involve emotions, so the more we have thought through issues and understand what is important to us and the people we are discussing them with ahead of time, the more likely we are to stay calm and present in the meeting.

Pay attention to how your body feels as you prepare for such a conversation. What sensations are you experiencing: Rapid heartbeat? Stomach ache? Sweating palms? Being in tune with these physical reactions, which are normal, helps us be in tune with our emotional responses. Preparation is a tool for calming our emotions since we have the time and space to use our thinking brain (prefrontal cortex) to reflect and develop talking points. As the conversation approaches, simple mindfulness techniques like taking a few deep breaths will lower strong emotional responses and cortisol levels, and allow you to show up calmer for the conversation.

Samir and Performance Review Preparation Samir, a senior leader for an international relief agency, confided in me during one of our coaching sessions that he hated doing performance reviews, particularly when the person's performance needed improvement. As we probed into this more, he realized he never felt fully prepared for these conversations. He admitted he was always in a rush and did not feel he had time to do more than skim the relevant documents just before meeting with the person. He recognized this was disrespectful to the person reporting to him, but also spending time gathering his thoughts, thinking about how to present them, and being clear on his messaging actually saved him time down the road. With ample preparation, up to an hour per person, he managed his performance reviews better; the next steps were clearer, accountability measures were spelled out, and employees left their reviews with the clarity to move forward.

Curiosity

Curiosity is at the core of navigating through a critical conversation. Some coaches encourage clients to focus on empathy but I think that is a high bar to set for many people. Rather, if you bring a curious mindset to a challenging conversation, you are set up for success because you arrive more open-minded, less fixed on holding a position or driving a specific decision. It also conveys humbleness because if you're curious to know what the other person feels and thinks, you are open to not having all the answers. Curiosity also implies patience and concern. One of the key ways to demonstrate curiosity is through open-ended questions such as "Tell me more . . ." or "I'm curious to understand . . . " or "What if . . . ?" In fact, open-ended questions are the fourth building block, but first let's talk about the third building block, active listening.

Deep Active Listening

The ability to develop and demonstrate active listening skills is a lifelong learning process for most of us. Deep and active listening means you absorb important information and the other person feels heard and seen. The good news is that everyone can build up and keep improving deep listening skills. I focus on four basic elements when I work with a client to improve their listening skills.

Commitment

Do you really want to listen? Can you slow down enough to focus on defining your listening intention? To develop better listening skills requires making it a priority. For instance, before having a conversation, tell yourself you are going to listen closely to the person speaking for a full two minutes, and you are going to jot down two or three questions to ask.

Eliminate Distractions

Turn off alerts on your screen. Put your phone away. Shut down your laptop, if possible. We know we can't fully listen if we are distracted. Most of us have a lot of control over how to minimize technology distractions. I once had a boss who would take calls when we were having one-on-one meetings. I was frustrated because I knew it would affect our ability to get through the list of issues I'd arrived with. More importantly, I felt deeply disrespected. And, no, I never said anything because I felt the power dynamics didn't allow for it.

Silence Isn't Golden

Active listening does not mean being silent. In fact, showing engagement through body language, such as head nodding, eye contact, and intermittently and appropriately saying phrases such as "I see" or "Tell me more" demonstrates engagement to the other person. This encourages them to continue because they sense your connection and focus.

Summary Is King

A key building block of deep active listening is the ability to summarize succinctly what the speaker said. "I am hearing you say that summer Fridays are an important part of our culture and we can work smart so we still meet all of our ambitious deadlines this summer." You have listened deeply enough to accurately summarize the information and this is validating for the speaker.[1] Additionally, it's an efficient way to ensure what they are saying is what you are understanding. That way, miscommunications can be caught quickly and not spiral out of control.

It's not just the words. Research tells us that much of what we communicate also is reflected in our body language and our tone.[2] Are you aware of the speaker's tone of voice? Is it loud or soft? Critical or warm? Can you experience any emotions through tone or body language? Are you aware of how they are holding themself? Are their arms crossed? Are they leaning into the conversation or leaning back? We can learn a lot about someone's comfort or discomfort by how they carry and conduct themselves when speaking to us. This skill takes practice, and I consider it a more advanced level of active listening. And in online meetings, it can be even more challenging to pick up these nonverbal cues.

These (very real!) examples are so outrageous that they are funny.

- A colleague who regularly cleans their nails with a pocketknife during meetings.
- A boss who has their back to Zoom meetings while they watch sports on another screen.
- A colleague who regularly pushes their chair back, folds their arms, and crosses their legs whenever they are frustrated by the direction a conversation was taking.

But nonverbal communication is serious and it contributes to people's perceptions of you. If you have a true and trusted colleague, why not ask them how you show up in meetings as a way to build your self-awareness.

How Jorge Improved His Listening Skills   Active listening requires focus, and focus is even more difficult for those with a diagnosis of ADHD. Jorge came to me after launching his second start-up because he had received feedback from his co-founder and team that he was slowing them down. They were frustrated because they kept having to revisit issues with him that he hadn't tuned into when they were discussed the first time, such as board meeting agendas, investor updates, and product release dates. Jorge had received an adult diagnosis of ADHD a couple of years earlier when he was 34 years old.

The first step was for Jorge to gather information from his colleagues about how his poor listening manifested itself and became a problem for him—and them. It turns out, Jorge didn't interrupt or speak out of turn, but colleagues accused him of selective hearing. For example, he would open up debate on decisions the team thought had been made. As we probed deeper, he realized his key issue was mentally moving in and out of the conversation because his mind wandered, often without warning. The result was that he missed important information in a conversation. Jorge tried several different strategies to keep engaged in meetings. He tried them one at a time, and some were more successful than others.

- He learned to ask a few open-ended questions as a way to stay engaged, such as "Tell me more . . ." and "I'm curious to hear. . ."
- He tried taking notes. The act of writing is a proven strategy to help some listen better. And pen and paper are superior for taking notes rather than using a laptop or iPad.[3]
- He started summarizing key points in meetings after critical conversation moments to ensure he absorbed the key takeaways.
- He decided that audio recordings of key meetings worked as an effective backup, but they were not an efficient way to recall information quickly.
- Finally, Jorge's team agreed to produce more detailed meeting minutes for Jorge to have a complete written record for reference.

Open-Ended Questions

I want you to better understand the power of open-ended questions. This is probably the easiest habit to build from this book and the one that will get you furthest in improving your communication skills.

When you use open-ended questions, you demonstrate curiosity, openness to new perspectives, and invite more participation rather than cutting it off. You invite your counterpart and/or meeting attendees to participate at a deeper level in the conversation at hand.

Examples of Open-Ended Questions

- I'm curious to hear what your thoughts are about that.
- What is possible?
- Can you tell me more about . . . ?
- What do you want us to explore?
- What if . . . ?
- What do you mean . . . ?
- What would it look like if . . . ?
- Great idea. What's our next step?

Tips on Using Open-Ended Questions

- Generally speaking, WHICH questions elicit yes/no and binary answers. They are at the bottom of the open-ended question hierarchy. WHO, WHEN, WHERE questions are better, and at the top of the hierarchy are WHY, HOW, and WHAT questions.
  - **How** do you feel about seeing a movie tonight?
  - **When** should we see a movie?
  - **Which** movie do you want to see?
- Context matters. Who is in the room and the issue under discussion will influence the types of open-ended questions that make the most sense. For instance, responding to fast-growing market demand for a product is very different from having to figure out what to do about an underperforming

brand. Open-ended questions are a good way to start in either case, but they need to be context specific.

- **What** do you believe is responsible for the growth in demand for our product?
- **How** did our product's demand fall so quickly after such strong sales last season?

- Do not get hung up if you use a question or statement to open up a conversation. For example, "tell me more" and "I'm curious about" are two of the most powerful conversation openers to deepen connection, possibility, and learning, and they are statements not questions.

- How a question is delivered is crucial. A semi-open-ended question delivered with humility and respect is more powerful than the most textbook-perfect open-ended question delivered in a flat tone or by a distracted person.

- If you stack your questions by firing them off one after another, even if they are open-ended, you won't be opening up the conversation. Active listening is even more important when you ask open-ended questions one at a time and allow people to respond.

Open-Ended Question Challenge

Put your top five go-to open-ended questions on a Post-it Note beside your monitor or beside your keyboard. Commit to using at least two open-ended questions in every meeting you participate in, and see for yourself how that opens up conversations—notice the increased depth, breadth, and participation that results.

Reflection Questions

- Which of the four building blocks for a challenging conversation is a priority for you to develop further?
- What is a concrete next step that you can take to develop that skill further?
- Are you aware of how your body feels when you are contemplating a challenging conversation? How can that body awareness help you as you prepare for the conversation?

Resources

- *Power Cues: The Subtle Science of Leading Groups, Persuading Others, and Maximizing Your Personal Impact* by Nick Morgan, Harvard Business Review Press (2014). I particularly like the discussion about the "second conversation" you hold with others every time you talk, that is, the power of the nonverbal messages you communicate to others, usually unknowingly.
- *The Coaching Habit: Say Less, Ask More & Change the Way You Lead Forever* by Michael Bungay Stanier, Page Two Books, Inc. (2016). Michael's book is friendly and comprehensive. It covers all four of these building blocks, and he includes numerous additional references for an even deeper dive into them.
- *Captivate: The Science of Succeeding with People* by Vanessa Van Edward, Penguin Publishing (2018). This practical book has many fun quizzes to test your people-reading skills. I also like how it is broken into sections based on first impressions and longer-term impressions.

9

COIN Framework: How to Have a Critical Conversation

I would rather have questions that can't be answered than answers that can't be questioned.

—Richard Feynman

COIN (Common Purpose, Observations, Inquiry, Next Steps) is the most versatile communication framework I know.[1] I introduce it to all my clients because every one of them has critical conversations during the timeframe that we work together and long afterward. This chapter builds on the evergreen work done by several authors who wrote the bestseller *Crucial Conversations: Tools for Talking When Stakes are High*. It's on its third edition, which gives you an idea of how timeless and relevant this framework is.

What COIN Is and When to Use It

The COIN framework gives you the tools to frame and structure a critical conversation—crucial when stakes are high, emotions run strong, and opinions differ. COIN has two phases: **preparation** and **activation**, and I delve into each of these phases in detail in the following pages. COIN lightens the cognitive load of conversations that you know will be emotionally demanding and require a lot of active listening. I like to think about COIN the same way you might use a recipe. COIN gives you the structure and confidence, so you can create the magic by adding your own creative touches. As you learn COIN, I invite you to think about everything you bring to the conversation as ingredients. COIN is your basic recipe to adapt and vary as you get more experienced with the techniques and process. COIN also helps you focus on the conversation unfolding and the other people participating in it.

Preparation for COIN[2]

We prepare for a challenging conversation with a balance of toughness and softness. We use the four building blocks from Chapter 8 to help us bring a balanced perspective to the conversation—not too "tough," that is, set in your way of viewing the issue one way. And not too "soft," that is, shying away from saying the hard things that need to be said. *Soft* also means you remain open and curious to hear the other side of the story.

How do you default in your uncomfortable conversations? Most of us tend toward either a tough or soft approach, and it's helpful to know which way we naturally lean. An effective conversation requires us to hold space for both tough and soft tendencies.

A softer perspective emphasizes emotions and feelings and the relationship.

- **What is important about this relationship?**
- **What do I really want to be different?**

A tougher perspective means you stand up straight and are clear about what you want to say and are invested in a concrete goal/outcome.

- **What is my position?**
- **How can I share my position without blame or defensiveness?**
- **What is not negotiable here?**

To bring both the soft and tough aspects to the conversation, ask yourself these questions.

- **Am I clear and focused on my goal?**
- **What might take me away from my goal and back to my place of comfort (either softness or toughness)?**
- **Am I more committed to my goal than to easing my discomfort?**

An example of approaching a conversation from **too tough** a perspective is: "You just aren't a strategic thinker. I've given you opportunities to do this work and you're not cutting it."

And **too soft** an approach: "I was going to ask how you feel about the work you're doing but things seem better. Why don't we talk about that new project on the horizon for your team?"

An example of a **balanced** approach is: "I appreciate the hard work you've been doing and I know you've been picking up others' slack. At the same time, my sense is that you're avoiding doing the more strategic work because it's harder for you. I want to understand if that is the case and how I can support you."

Having this self-awareness of how you tend to show up in a conversation can be very powerful. Remember, we are looking for a perspective that balances the two.

You have prepared for the conversation. You know how you want to approach it. And now you are ready for the conversation itself!

Activation of COIN

You want to launch the conversation with a common purpose. You have some observations, not assumptions, to share. You recognize the importance of asking questions, of truly listening to the other person's perspective. And you are committed to concluding the conversation with clarity about what comes next, and the accountability that implies on both sides. Table 9.1 presents a snapshot of how to activate COIN in real time.

Lenny Decides to Leave His Job　　Lenny was hired by Carla, the founder of a rapidly growing cosmetics firm, as its creative director. Lenny thought he knew what to expect in this role—a team of 12, a growing budget, and an opportunity to stage a number of live events with its flagship retail partners. But when he joined the company, it was undergoing a massive reorganization since sales the previous year had been dramatically lower than expected. Lenny found himself with an unhappy team half the size, a smaller budget than anticipated, and a lot of stress.

Very quickly, he knew the role was not a good fit for him and decided to leave after nine months on the job. Lenny's **goal** was to inform his boss he had decided to leave, and soon. He was simultaneously concerned about irreparably damaging the relationship he greatly valued, and suspected he might find himself persuaded by the charismatic founder to stay and give it another try. The COIN framework came in very handy.

The **common purpose** was: "We both want this company to have the best creative director for this role in place."

Table 9.1 COIN Explained.

C – Common Purpose. You want to create positive alignment with the other person around something you both value.	• What is the shared importance of this conversation? • What shared goals do we have? • Why does this conversation matter to us?
O – Observations. This is the starting point. The facts. Both people need the opportunity to present the facts as they understand them. And this is where active listening skills are critical.	• How do I present my version of the facts and data? • How do I invite the other person to share their observations? • Can I use "I" statements to help keep my assumptions and generalizations in check?
I – Inquiry. This naturally flows from the facts. We want a dance between sharing observations and investigating motivations, feelings, conflicts, rationales. In real life, it may not be this linear.	• How can I get curious and stay that way? • Am I listening, *really* listening? • Am I assuming positive intent? • Which open-ended questions best serve me here? • How am I ensuring this is a conversation and not a monologue?
N – Next Steps. The easiest and shortest step. A great conversation can be wasted if there isn't alignment on next steps. We want the momentum to build toward resolution.	• Who is doing what, by when, and how will you know? • Do you need to schedule a follow-up meeting?

Lenny's **observations** were that his job expectations were different from the reality he encountered, and he had several clear examples of this, including the vastly reduced budget and team size.

To prepare for the **inquiry** phase, we spent time anticipating the kinds of responses he should expect from Carla and how to prepare for them. We discussed the value of pausing and asking open-ended questions to check in on how she felt, and her observations.

It turned out to be a very painful conversation. Carla was upset and angry, and felt that Lenny was abandoning her when she needed him most. For Carla, "I thought I'd found a true creative partner to help me refocus and redirect the brand. I can't tell you how disappointed I am."

Lenny listened. Lenny talked about his mixed feelings. "I love the brand and I wanted to help it soar even higher, but at this point in my career, I'm not prepared to do the work of junior designers because of budget challenges." He also shared additional observations about the qualities, characteristics, and career stage he believed would be a more successful profile in this role. He found a way to balance the soft and hard perspectives needed.

They ended up agreeing to have another conversation as the **next step**, after the weekend. They fixed that meeting time and date before ending their current meeting. The next week, emotions were not running as high and they identified clear next steps about how to communicate the news to Lenny's team, and to launch the search process.

This is an example of a critical conversation where one person was already clear on a decision, and wanted to keep that goal in focus, but wanted to present the decision kindly, thoughtfully, and humanely. It required an additional conversation to have Carla absorb and accept the decision more fully.

In Lenny's words: "I knew it was the right decision for me to leave but that didn't make the conversations with Carla any easier. The COIN framework helped lighten my anxiety because I had a structure to utilize and keep returning to when the conversation got highly charged emotionally."

Lenny landed a creative director role at a luxury accessory company, and he felt it was a much better fit. Carla found a new creative director who was earlier in her career and excited by the prospect of helping build the brand to support the company turnaround and the product refocus.

Tips for Utilizing COIN in Real Life

- Critical conversations are about reconciling your stories with the actual facts, so you and your counterpart can get on the same page about what is going on.
- The balance between "soft" versus" tough" depends on what the content of the conversation is—are you having a probing conversation to understand a situation better or are you delivering difficult, definitive news?
- The beginning, common purpose, and end, next steps, of this recipe are straightforward. The challenging part can be the dance between observation and inquiry. That pathway is not always linear. You may share observations on both sides, probe what they mean through open-ended questions, and then bring up other facts that require further discussion before you arrive at next steps.
- Many critical conversations are not easily resolved in one conversation, the next step may be to continue the conversation, remembering to line up in advance the time and date as your next step.

Reflection Questions

- What is the uncomfortable conversation you need to have? What makes it so uncomfortable?
- What is at risk if you don't have it?
- How can you prepare for a critical conversation with a balance between "soft" and "tough"?
- What is the value of applying the COIN model?

Resources

- *Crucial Conversations: Tools for Talking When Stakes Are High, 3rd Ed.* by Joseph Grenny, Ron McMillan, Kerry Patterson, Al Switzler, Emily Gregory, McGraw Hill (2022). If you want a deeper dive into themes covered in this chapter, this book is an excellent resource. I particularly like their six-minute preparation protocol.
- *Difficult Conversations: How to Discuss What Matters Most* by Douglas Stone, Bruce Patten, and Sheila Heen, Penguin Publishing (2010). This book comes out of Harvard's Negotiation Project and has a strong emphasis on negotiation, persuasion, and influence tactics. One White House administration made it required reading for its top 1,600 political appointees!

10

Communicate FOR: A Framework Focused on Relationships

Peace is not the absence of conflict but the ability to cope with it.
—Mahatma Gandhi

Lean on this framework when the relationship is more important than the actual conflict or achieving a particular outcome. Marshall Rosenberg's work on nonviolent communication is the bedrock of this conflict resolution approach. Don't expect to use Communicate FOR (Focused On Relationships) when you are shopping for a used car or negotiating the sale of your company!

The Communicate FOR framework has the potential to profoundly impact both personal and professional relationships because it (gently) forces us to confront our needs, and communicate them clearly and kindly.

Empathy is critical in how we respond to conflict. It requires us to focus full attention on the other person's message. Generating empathy requires that we give to others the time and space they need to express themselves fully and to feel understood. Yes, in Chapter 8 I suggested it was enough for you to bring curiosity to a challenging conversation. But Communicate FOR is a challenging framework that is more successful when you understand what others are experiencing. In the words of Marshall Rosenberg, "empathy calls upon us to empty our mind and listen to others with our whole being."[1]

This framework is helpful both for expressing yourself and understanding the feelings and needs of others. When someone communicates negatively with us, we have four options:

- Blame ourselves.
- Blame others.
- Sense our own feelings and needs.
- Sense the feelings and needs within the other person's negative message.

The fourth option requires practice and builds on the third. Needs have to be identified on both sides before we choose strategies to meet our individual needs. As you get more skilled at using Communicate FOR, you can use it in a conflictual situation that has a lot of back and forth, and where you are focused on both sets of needs being met. It's a dance based on the relationship's importance.

This simple but deceptively challenging framework requires a lot of practice. The focus in this chapter is on expressing yourself since that is the first step to understanding the framework's power.

Communicate FOR Explained

Communicate FOR reframes how we **express** ourselves, how we **hear** others, and **resolve** conflicts by focusing our awareness on what we are seeing, feeling, needing, and requesting.

Seeing

We first need to focus on observable behaviors that affect us without mixing in evaluation. We know there is a difference between an observation and our evaluation of what we observe. When we combine observation with evaluation, people tend to hear criticism, and that isn't helpful in resolving conflict.

Feelings

Allowing ourselves to be vulnerable by expressing our feelings is another part of resolving conflict. But many of us are taught that feelings are private and should not be expressed, particularly at work. Common negative feelings are mad, sad, tired, scared, frustrated, and confused (vs. peaceful, loving, glad, playful, interested).

Needs

This is the most challenging aspect of the framework. We often have trouble articulating a feeling, let alone understanding what the unmet need is behind it. Most of us have never been taught to think in terms of our own needs. We tend to think about what is wrong with other people when our needs aren't fulfilled. The goal is to move from blaming someone else to expressing clearly what we need. If we express our needs, we have a better chance of getting them met. The more directly we can connect our feelings to our needs, the easier it is for others to respond in a way that can satisfy us.

Categories of universal human needs include desires for connection, empathy, community, self-expression, well-being, safety, creativity, and meaning. Each of these categories covers specific needs. For instance, the category of connection includes: affection, closeness, companionship, kindness, intimacy, nurturing, and respect.

Asks

We also need to learn how to make specific requests that are accurately heard by the other person. Requests are received as demands if the other person believes they will be blamed or punished if they do not comply. We are not asking someone to change their behavior to get our own way; rather, we want to establish relationships based on honesty and empathy that will eventually lead to both parties' needs being filled. Since resolving conflict is a two-way street, we seek to fulfill our needs only once we have identified the needs of both parties.

Tony and Dwayne Get Better at Getting Along   I worked with the product and engineering department heads at a tech company whose problematic relationship was impacting their teams and the company overall. We used Communicate FOR to help them find a way to understand each other's perspectives and needs, and to provide them with a tool to use when tensions escalated.

Tony, the product head, was new to the company, and felt frustrated because he wanted recognition for how he'd jumped in and made significant contributions quickly. Dwayne, the tech lead, was a long-tenured employee who felt angry because he wanted respect from his new colleague for all the processes he'd built over time. Dwayne lived in Nevada; Tony was based in New Jersey and had been hired during Covid. These tensions were complicated by the challenges of remote work and the company's decision to remain fully virtual post-Covid.

They didn't become best friends, but they did navigate a healthier relationship when they expressed their feelings, understood each other's needs, and held each other accountable to act differently. Dwayne agreed to articulate more appreciation in meetings and to start emails with positive acknowledgments, such as calling out deadlines met and product roadmap enhancements. Tony agreed to consult with Dwayne before making any decisions that would affect engineering, such as moving up product deadlines to meet sales requests. They agreed on the need to both be on the same page about what was working and what could be improved.

As Dwayne said, "Tony and I found a way to understand each other better and that led to a better working relationship. And consistently trying to understand each other's needs has meant that we could better work out the kinks in how the engineering and product departments work together. And at the end of the day, we both want to be respected for our hard work and expertise. I keep reminding myself to act on that. It seems to be working!"

Andy, the CEO who initially engaged me, was so impressed with how Dwayne and Tony turned it around that he asked me to run a workshop at their company offsite to introduce the Communicate FOR framework to the entire staff. After the offsite he said, "We all walked away from that workshop better equipped to deal with our colleagues' feelings and needs. Key for me was learning to listen in such a way that I could better differentiate between a feeling and a need."

Communicate FOR at a Glance

Table 10.1 lays out the framework's four elements and how to use them in a conversation. The third column highlights the value these elements bring to a challenging conversation. The final two columns list examples showing when the framework's structure is used correctly and incorrectly.

Canceled Contract A client canceled my contract without any discussion as I was about to start it.

"Fred, you informed me by email that my coaching engagement with Jerome was on hold, four hours before our first meeting." (**see**) I am uncomfortable (**feel**) about such a big change with so little notice. I would like to (**desire**) collaborate

Table 10.1 Communicate FOR at a Glance.

4 Elements of the Framework	Structure	Value of Using the Elements and Structure	Correct Examples	Incorrect Examples
See. Observations I make that affect me.	"When I see you..."	▪ No judgments, no generalizations ▪ Just observable behaviors ▪ Don't assume you know intent and try not to evaluate.	▪ You arrived late to our team huddle the last three days. ▪ Henry yelled at his team very loudly.	▪ You always arrive late. ▪ Henry is aggressive.
Feel. How I feel in relation to what I observe.	"I feel..."	▪ Acknowledge that sharing feelings is tough, and you may not feel safe. ▪ Feelings are different than thoughts. ▪ What others do may stimulate my feelings, but they are caused by my unmet needs. ▪ If I allow myself to be vulnerable by expressing my feelings, it can help to resolve conflict.	▪ I'm sad that you are moving to another firm. ▪ When you look at your phone when talking to me, I feel lonely.	▪ I think your move to another firm will be a challenge for me. ▪ When you talk to me and look at your phone, I feel neglected.

| **Desire.** The needs/desires/values that create my feelings. | "Because I want/need/value/would like. . ." | <ul><li>I feel the way that I do because I have an unmet need or desire.</li><li>I need to own that need/desire.</li><li>I can't blame anyone else for that need or desire being unmet.</li><li>We judge others when we aren't in touch with our own needs and desires.</li><li>Judgments, criticisms, diagnoses, and interpretations of others are misguided expressions of our own needs and values.</li></ul> | <ul><li>I feel frustrated when you arrive late because I was hoping we would have time to review our presentation before the client meeting.</li><li>I feel angry when you say that because I want your respect and I hear your words as an insult.</li></ul> | <ul><li>I feel frustrated because you are always late and it is so inconsiderate.</li><li>You make me angry when you say that, because you are constantly insulting me.</li></ul> |

(Continued)

Table 10.1 (Continued)

4 Elements of the Framework	Structure	Value of Using the Elements and Structure	Correct Examples	Incorrect Examples
Ask. The concrete actions I request to enrich my life and your life.	"Would you be willing to. . ."	▪ My request to you to enrich each of our lives ▪ My request uses positive action language, not vague language ▪ The clearer I am about what I want, and the clearer I express my want, the more likely it is I will get it.	▪ I'd like you to agree to knock on my bedroom door before entering. ▪ I want you to tell me how I handled leading the All Hands meeting – what worked well and what you'd like me to do differently next time.	▪ Would you try to start respecting my privacy? ▪ I'd like you to be honest with me about yesterday's All Hands meeting.

with you to find a solution that works for both of us. Would you be open to jumping on a call this week (**ask**) to brainstorm options so that the work can continue?

Fred and I had a call, and he apologized for the lack of notice and the rationale for postponing the work. We agreed to revisit the start of the engagement in a month. The coaching started shortly after that.

Online College Tours During Covid, my junior in high school did not do virtual online college tours, as we'd agreed he would. "You have only done two virtual college tours and you said you'd complete all twelve by the end of spring break." (**see**) "I'm anxious (**feel**) about your lack of progress on this task that we'd agreed on. I want the peace of mind (**desire**) to know that when you say you'll do something that it gets done, particularly around the college process which is stressful at the best of times. I would like us to set aside time tomorrow to discuss what's getting in the way for you and how we can move this important "to do" forward to completion (**ask**).

This conversation was the beginning of a longer conversation. I listened to his responses and encouraged him to use this framework. I actively listened to his feelings and needs. It turns out that he felt very disconnected from the college application process in general during Covid, and we came up with strategies to improve his engagement, while validating his feelings and desires.

Communicate FOR is both a framework and a process. I want you to feel empowered to go off and try using it after reading this chapter. It is a simple process that you need to practice to hone your skills. Why don't you start by completing the following exercise.

Communicate FOR Exercise

See how powerful Communicate FOR is for yourself in this simple reflection exercise.

Uncensored Message. Think of someone who makes life less than wonderful (challenging, conflictual) for you and write down, uncensored, what you would like to say to them.

Alternate Message Using Communicate FOR Framework

1. Write down what the person says or does (**see**).
2. Write how you feel when the person speaks or acts in the way described (**feel**).
3. Write your need in relation to how the person speaks or acts (**desire**).
4. Imagine you are talking directly to the person and express a request in the form of, "I would like you to . . ." (**ask**).
5. **Now put it all together** using this form: When I see/ hear . . . I feel . . . because I want. . . . Would you be willing to . . . ?

Ask Yourself

- What worked about the framework/what didn't?
- Could you imagine using it in "real life"? Why or why not?
- How can you practice using this framework in your daily life?

Reflection Questions

- Is there a conflictual situation in your life where using the Communicate FOR framework may help resolve conflict?
- Could you use this framework to understand the other person's perspective in this conflict?
- If you aren't comfortable using this framework in live interactions, can you use it as a reflection tool to better understand your perspective or to plan a conversation?

Resources

- *Nonviolent Communication, Third Edition*, by Marshall Rosenberg, PuddleDancer Press (2015). He was the pioneer in the field of nonviolent communication, and these techniques have been deployed in some very challenging situations such as interventions with inner-city gangs and Israeli-Palestinian negotiations, where both sides seemed unwavering in their perspectives and viewpoints. Facilitators, coaches, and therapists can get certified in this methodology. https://www.cnvc.org/learn-nvc
- "A Mindful Approach to Nonviolent Communication with Oren Jay Sofer," podcast (Nov. 2019). A master meditation instructor intersects mindfulness with nonviolent communication tools. https://scottbarrykaufman.com/podcast/a-mindful-approach-to-nonviolent-communication-with-oren-jay-sofer/
- *Your Complete Nonviolent Communication Guide.* This is a user-friendly guide to the principles and application of this framework. https://positivepsychology.com/non-violent-communication/

11

Compassionate Candor Framework

Honesty is love.

—Arthur C. Brooks

I want us to reframe feedback into compassionate candor. If someone's actions are successful, as a boss, you should reinforce them. And if someone's actions are problematic, you should let them know, and support them to improve. Candor should be built on compassion. I see it as an act of love, actually.

Bosses are uncomfortable delivering feedback for the most part, so they avoid doing it. This makes sense: our brains are programmed to avoid conflict unless it's a direct threat to our safety. If we are feeling safe and working productively, why introduce tension and possible conflict?[1] And yet, as bosses, we should not shy away from feedback.

My framework owes a lot to the research and strategies outlined by Kim Scott in her book *Radical Candor*.[2] She opened up the conversation about feedback to show that we can bring a more human-centric philosophy to the topic without losing sight of business realities.

Compassionate Candor: Two Key Dimensions

We all know a boss who is too direct and rubs us the wrong way. We also all know a boss who is too conflict-avoidant to give us the feedback that we want or need. Compassionate candor shows us how we can combine these two dimensions into a winning approach for delivering and receiving feedback.

Compassionate

You need a trusting, compassionate relationship with the people who work for you to deliver feedback that lands. I emphasize three keys on how to build a compassionate relationship.

- **Complete person.** Invest in knowing the complete person. You want to accept and know them as whole people with rich and complex lives outside of work, as well as understanding their strengths and areas for development on the job. According to Kim Scott, "We are all humans and we are all trying to do our best, and we all face different challenges. We bring our whole selves to work." You don't have to know every detail, but you should have some understanding of who your employees are and what their lives are like outside of work.
  - Whom do they live with?
  - What do they do for fun?
  - How old are their parents? Their children?
- **Context.** Pay attention to where and when you deliver feedback. As a rule of thumb, constructive feedback is best delivered in private; affirming feedback can be delivered in public, though introverted folks may still prefer it delivered in private.

- **Connection to motivation.** Understand what motivates people you manage because feedback is most effective when it connects to someone's motivation. Common motivators include: achievement, power, affiliation, security, and adventure.[3]

The main way to develop compassion is through conversation both informally and in your one-on-ones. (We cover the importance of one-on-ones in Chapter 13.) It also means being available when people who work for you need your support, even if it isn't at the most convenient moment for you.

Candor

You need to deliver direct feedback. No one should walk away after receiving feedback and be unclear about the message they received.

- **Clear.** Your feedback should be direct, actionable, and never mean-spirited. You base feedback on observations, not generalizations. Feedback is specific.
- **Challenge.** Your feedback should be challenging because we want to push our people to do better. But you can't challenge directly if you haven't built trust. We want to ease our employees out of their comfort zones in order to grow. We also want to offer our support to help them respond to feedback. The challenge can't outpace the person.
- **Comfort.** As a boss, you, too, must be comfortable receiving feedback. That also helps create a relationship of trust. This is an important muscle to build. As a boss, you need to be thankful for any feedback regardless of how it is delivered. However, as a boss, you need to be extremely thoughtful about how you deliver feedback to others.

Two Categories of Feedback: Affirming and Constructive

When we think of the word *feedback*, most people associate it with something negative. No! Feedback is both affirming and constructive. And the ratio of affirming to constructive matters.

Affirming

Affirming feedback reinforces to someone that you want them to repeat specific actions/behaviors in the future.

- I like how you took charge and got the team to meet that client deadline.
- I appreciated you reviewing my presentation and giving me those suggestions to improve the flow.

Constructive

Constructive feedback is what we primarily think about when we think about feedback, it's commonly referred to as criticism. I want to change that mindset!

- When you show up late to our meetings, team members feel like you aren't respecting their time.
- Your emails to our clients are not hitting the right tone. I have a few examples with me that show how we want to communicate with them to make them feel we are both responsive and highly professional.

While there is some debate about the ratio of affirming to constructive feedback, in my experience a 3:1 ratio is about right. In other words, for every four times you deliver feedback to someone, three of those times should be affirming, and one time should be constructive. In other words, affirming feedback should vastly outweigh the constructive.

The ratio is important because the affirmative feedback contributes to building a positive, trusting connection between you and the other person. In neuroscience terms, these are some of the positive aspects of in-group effects on the brain and behaviors.[4] They are, then, more positively disposed to trust you, and will be more open to hear and respond to constructive feedback.

I like to think of feedback as frequent afternoon snacks, whereas a performance review is a three-course meal for special occasions. Feedback should happen frequently and not be a big deal. It can be an interaction lasting just a few minutes.

The Basics of Delivering Compassionate Candid Feedback

Candid feedback that lands well needs to be delivered within the context of a trusting compassionate relationship. Once you have that base of trust, you should deliver feedback with candor, patience, and optimism (Table 11.1). Without a base of trust, candid feedback will be seen with suspicion and possibly resentment.

Some clients have commented that this structure seems rigid. I agree: it's a bare-bones recipe focused on candor. Use it as a baseline, then experiment with it and add your own creativity, personality, and empathy. The key is to build a trusting relationship with the person *before* delivering candid feedback. That way, they'll receive what you say better and will be more open to listening to it and incorporating your suggestions.

A Leader Can't Always Be a Nice Person   Ali is a nice guy who admits to wanting everyone to like him. He also is CEO of a growing productivity platform that has scaled to several

Table 11.1 Four Steps to Deliver Compassionate Candid Feedback.

Step	Why?	Examples
Permission: ask permission to give feedback	Get their attention and focus.	• Are you available for some quick feedback? • Is now a good time to catch up? • Can we please have a quick debrief?
Observations: describe the recent behavior	Focus on observable behavior, not intentions and not generalizations.	• When you arrive late for our staff meetings. . . • When you fail to copy the entire team on messages. . . • When you roll your eyes in meetings and interrupt others when they are speaking. . .
Impact: describe the result/impact	Bring attention to the impact the person's action/behavior has on the work, the team or both.	• . . . the entire team is frustrated because we have to repeat ourselves to bring you up to speed. • . . . we have communication breakdowns that are impacting our ability to meet deadlines. • . . . team members have let me know that they feel disrespected.
Ask: describe the behavior change you are requesting	In some cases, end feedback at the third step (impact); other times, clarify your "ask" with the fourth step.	• Could you please attend staff meetings on time? If you know you'll be late, let someone know ahead of time. • Going forward, ensure that everyone is copied, okay? • Please control those behaviors at meetings; would you like me to check in after meetings to provide some quick feedback?

hundred employees very quickly. A lot of Ali's and my work has been about delivering feedback faster and more directly. Earlier in the company's history, Ali avoided giving feedback to his staff until problems were so far gone that people ended up exiting the firm. Ali has worked hard to build up his feedback delivery muscle. We focused on building his awareness about his leadership responsibilities, and how to overcome the need to be liked by everyone. What motivated him most, however, were exit interviews of departing employees, some of whom were bitter about his lack of candor and how that had affected their confidence and motivation in their roles. "That really hit home hard and I knew I needed to change for the sake of my employees and their job satisfaction. Compassionate candor is not always my first reaction, but I am learning and I am getting better at it, and the feedback to me about delivering clear feedback has energized me."

Compassionate Candor: Key Tips

- The delivery of feedback is an act of love and a key responsibility of every boss.
- Recognize that we come to the workplace as whole people with rich, complicated, and often challenging lives outside of work. A trusting relationship grounded in compassion and mutual respect is needed for the person to "hear" and act on constructive feedback.
- We hold our colleagues and reportees to high standards of accountability because we believe in their abilities and potential.
- Remember the ratio of 3:1 affirming to constructive feedback.
- Candid feedback is specific, direct, and actionable.
- We get better at compassionate candor by exercising this muscle, and recognizing this is a journey of continuous improvement, not a destination.

Reflection Questions

- How do you feel about giving feedback to your team members, colleagues, and boss?
- Does reframing feedback through the lens of compassionate candor make sense to you?
- What steps can you take to make this mindset shift?
- How can you operationalize compassionate candor at work and in the rest of your life?
- How can you build on the basic feedback building blocks to have them suit your style for delivering compassionate candor?

Resources

- *HBR Guide to Delivering Effective Feedback* edited by Amy Gallo (HBR Guide Series) Paperback (2016). I like this book because it delivers a variety of perspectives from numerous experts on how to deliver feedback—positive and constructive, short-term and long-term.
- *Radical Candor* by Kim Scott, St. Martin's Press (2017). The Radical Candor framework developed by Kim Scott demonstrates how powerful feedback can be when it integrates caring personally with challenging directly. Compassionate candor draws its inspiration from her framework, and the second edition of her book recommended using compassionate candor instead of radical candor. I highly recommend both her books *Radical Candor* and *Just Work* (2021), which emphasizes diversity, equity, and inclusion.
- "A Complete List of Feedback Models" (2021) on Saberr .com. A list of simple, highly actionable feedback models. (https://blog.saberr.com/how-to-give-good-feedback)

12

The Conversation Funnel Framework

There are no secrets to success. It is the result of preparation, hard work, and learning from failure

—Colin Powell

We have different kinds of conversations with our peers, our teams, and our bosses, ranging from blue sky brainstorming to definitive decision making, and everything in between. The Conversation Funnel is a simple framework to help you appropriately prepare for and engage in an important conversation or meeting.

The Conversation Funnel Explained

The Conversation Funnel is not a decision-making framework. Rather, it is a framework that helps you orient what stage a conversation is at and helps you answer the question: What kind of conversation should I be prepared to have? If you know a meeting is about exploring issues or narrowing down options, or at the other extreme, making decisions, then you have an

Objectives

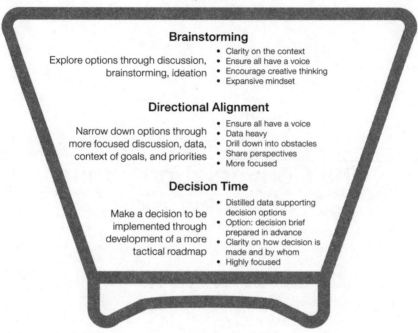

Brainstorming

Explore options through discussion, brainstorming, ideation
- Clarity on the context
- Ensure all have a voice
- Encourage creative thinking
- Expansive mindset

Directional Alignment

Narrow down options through more focused discussion, data, context of goals, and priorities
- Ensure all have a voice
- Data heavy
- Drill down into obstacles
- Share perspectives
- More focused

Decision Time

Make a decision to be implemented through development of a more tactical roadmap
- Distilled data supporting decision options
- Option: decision brief prepared in advance
- Clarity on how decision is made and by whom
- Highly focused

Figure 12.1   The Conversation Funnel.

important perspective and context. Now you are ready to answer these two questions:

- How can I best *prepare* for this meeting?
- How can I optimally *engage* in this conversation/meeting? Specifically, the types of questions you ask, how data is used, and how to analyze options.

The Conversation Funnel in Action

Refer to the Conversation Funnel graphic (Figure 12.1) when you know a critical meeting or conversation is on the horizon, and you want to be well-prepared either to run or participate in the meeting. I have found this framework particularly helpful working with technical experts and neurodiverse leaders whose communication skills need improving, particularly those who struggle to pick up colleagues' social cues in meetings.

This framework can also be used at the beginning of a meeting as a checklist for direction.

- Are we all clear on the meeting's context?
- Are we clear on where this meeting is situated in the conversation funnel?
- Are we clear on the meeting's specific goal?

I developed the Conversation Funnel when I worked with my client Zack, and I've used it successfully with a number of clients since then.

Zack Discovers How the Conversation Funnel Can Help

Zack is a software engineer who had joined a rapidly scaling tech company as the chief technology officer several months earlier. He kept receiving feedback from the CEO that his participation in meetings was missing the mark and alienating colleagues. As we grappled to understand what was going on, Zack realized he approached all meetings with the same intention: get decisions made as fast as possible so that he could get on with building whatever was needed.

Zack recounted to me that he just wanted everyone and everything to keep moving. "There is so much work to be done, so much code to write. The faster we make decisions, the better for me and my team."

Once we started categorizing meetings as falling into the top, middle, or bottom of the Conversation Funnel, he began to see that engaging differently would be more effective and result in less frustration all around. He created a three-step checklist:

1. Determine where the meeting fits in the Conversation Funnel.
2. Clarify the meeting's context and specific goals.
3. Draw on a go-to list of questions that align to each of the three phases of the Conversation Funnel.

This checklist helped him situate the meeting in his mind, and ultimately, how to think about his participation. For instance, he also found himself enjoying cross-team meetings more when he understood that ideas were being shared but decisions weren't being made.

In Zack's words: "It is a little embarrassing that I needed a framework to help me figure out that different types of conversations happen at different types of meetings. Oh well, the main point is that I've gotten better at asking the right kinds of questions, and not being shy about asking for clarity if I'm unclear about a meeting's purpose."

The Conversation Funnel is a versatile tool because it can help you prepare the agenda for a meeting, or help you personally prepare for a meeting that you'll be participating in. Finally, it's useful during a meeting as an accountability tool to ensure folks stay on track—whether its brainstorming, narrowing down a set of options, or making final decisions. I think of it as multipurpose scaffolding.

Reflection Questions

- Before you participate in a conversation or meeting, are you clear where it sits in the Conversation Funnel? If not, can this framework assist you to ask the right questions (e.g., context, process) to find out?
- Once you position the conversation, what kinds of questions should you think about asking? And what kind of preparation is required for that conversation?

IV

Unlocking the Keys to Great Management

For managers this part is required reading because you are responsible for setting up your direct reports and teams for success, and removing roadblocks in their way. For everyone else, these frameworks and tactics help you see the world from your boss's or client's perspective, and to navigate being a successful team member. They also will help prepare you to lead your own team one day soon.

We start with the basics in Chapter 13 and focus on how to manage your individual direct reports. It's actually a meta-framework because I share additional tools, checklists, and recipes specific to each of the **Four Keys to Great Management**.

Chapters 14 and 15 are focused on **team management**. In Chapter 14, I walk through the **GRPI** framework (Goals, Roles and Responsibilities, Processes, and Interpersonal Relationships). It is a 50-year-old framework still young at heart!

Strong teams are key to an organization's success. In Chapter 15, I present the **Six Keys to Unlock the Power of a Strong Team**. It is based on the important work developed by author and management consultant Patrick Lencioni over the past 20 years. This is my go-to framework when I coach teams because of its accessibility and versatility.

13

Four Keys to Great Management: A Meta-Framework

Corporate culture matters. How management chooses to treat its people impacts everything—for better or for worse.

—Simon Sinek

Like so many experiences in life, becoming a great manager is a journey more than a destination.

Entire books are written about the difference between managers and leaders. For our purposes, I differentiate between a manager and leader as follows: a leader doesn't necessarily have direct reports but a manager always does. And a leader is about challenging the status quo while a manager tries to maintain or achieve it.[1] The focus here is on management, though it often goes hand in hand with leadership.

Even if you have good instincts for managing others, experience, skills training, and coaching are just as important, particularly for new managers. What follows is for new managers, but even the most seasoned manager will find this to be a helpful refresher.

The four management basics in Table 13.1 ensure that anyone who works for you will understand their roles and

Table 13.1   Four Keys to Great Management.

1: BUILD TRUST: Create a relationship of trust through regular check-ins.	**3: GIVE FEEDBACK:** Communicate clearly about how staff performed.
2: DELEGATE: Communicate clearly about what staff needs to do.	**4: COACH:** Develop your staff's potential in this role and for their next role through performance and career coaching.

Source: Adapted from Manager Tools. https://www.manager-tools.com/manager-tools-basics.

responsibilities, get feedback on their performance, and get coaching for professional growth in both their current role and future career goals. And all of this needs to build on a relationship of trust.[2]

Key 1: Create Trust through Regular Check-Ins

Regular one-on-one check-ins are a key tool for you and your direct reports to develop a relationship of trust. They should be calendared well in advance and not shifted around unless absolutely necessary, held weekly or bi-weekly, and the length may vary from 30–60 minutes.

The staffer owns the agenda and knows they have your full attention on issues important to them. Updates are delivered and challenges brainstormed, but sometimes personal issues like eldercare challenges or stress about a child's college application may also be discussed. Don't underestimate your employees' desire to share personal issues that could affect their work life. You can only provide support, and potential assistance, when you know what they are struggling with.

We can see how critical it is to implement the effective conversation building blocks discussed in Chapter 8 during a one-on-one. The boss has to be fully present, ready to listen deeply, and ask open-ended questions. Both parties need to arrive curious and prepared.

Jamal Implements One-on-Ones to Build Trust Quickly   My client Jamal was promoted to SVP of operations at a large event production company and multiple departments now report to him. He was overwhelmed and concerned about how to manage some challenging personalities and keep current on numerous complex work projects such as a major awards ceremony and numerous fashion shows.

We agreed he would start having regular one-on-ones with his eight direct reports to build relationships and get closer to their work. Jamal was concerned about the amount of time he was going to spend weekly in these check-ins but agreed to try it for six months. He announced his intention to his staff in person and via email. He asked his assistant to deal with the scheduling and told him how important it was not to move these meetings around. Finally, he provided a template his direct reports could modify to prepare their meeting agenda.

It took a couple of months for the new format to gain traction. But when his direct reports realized Jamal showed up prepared and present, and didn't shift the check-ins around on his calendar, they began to engage more. By the sixth month, they were no longer seen as a "flavor of the month" initiative. They had become a normal and productive part of the work calendar.

Jamal managed to avert a couple of major supplier problems because he learned about the issues early through these one-on-ones. He also got to know his staff much better on an individual level and learned about their lives beyond work. Mutual trust and respect deepened more quickly than he had thought possible.

In Jamal's words, "I think my secret weapon in these meetings was that I always asked the question 'What is your biggest roadblock and what can I do to help?' When my reports saw that I was willing to help with challenges it really increased my credibility."

Jamal's staff also had positive reports. Anton, senior project manager, said, "I started to feel much more comfortable brainstorming with Jamal about challenges I was facing. He really showed up. And when I faced a crisis in my marriage, I felt comfortable letting him know. We didn't dwell on it but knowing he was aware and supportive was quite a relief."

Try These One-on-One Structures

The following are two examples of structures for one-on-one check-ins my clients use. Their differences reflect varying company cultures and personal styles. The agenda template can be as simple as a shared Google Doc or as sophisticated as an online human resource platform.[3]

The Basics

- Cadence: 30 minutes weekly.
- Emphasis: rapid snapshot from direct report's perspective.
- Staff person's update (10 minutes). They raise any issues on their mind, including where they need assistance from their manager.
- Boss's update (10 minutes). They may use the time to follow up on items from the previous check-in, to share organizational news or information critical to staffer's work, to provide feedback, to delegate a project or to ask open-ended questions about progress.
- Next steps (10 minutes). This includes items to be reviewed at the next check-in.

The Coaching Model

- Cadence: 1 hour bi-weekly.
- Emphasis: focus on coaching the staffer on resolving their challenges.
- The good (10 minutes). A few positive things that have happened at work and/or personally since last one-on-one.
- Issues: (30 minutes). Staff person prepares two or three work-related issues, including personal issues is optional. The staffer details the issue, proposed solution, and next actions. The manager coaches them on how to resolve the issues.
- Goals (5 minutes). A quick reaffirmation of quarterly goals to re-emphasize the three key goals the staffer should care about.
- Other topics, feedback, and next steps (15 minutes). Additional topics the staff person or boss want to discuss, feedback to each other, and next steps.

Key 2: Delegate So Everyone Can Grow

Many of my clients complain they have no time to think strategically because they are too busy. Yet they often are so busy because they are not effective delegators. Reasons range from a lack of trust to guilt about overloading their already very busy team members. Nonetheless, if a boss doesn't develop strong delegation skills, they will be consistently in the weeds and denying their direct reports the opportunity to develop their skills and get their accomplishments noticed.

Effective delegation is specific; it has a beginning, middle, and end, and the level of delegation is clearly understood by both parties.

A Delegated Task Is Specific and SMARTER

The SMARTER acronym sums up perfectly the parameters of successful delegation. The boss and the person to whom the project is delegated can use this checklist to ensure everyone is set up for success.

- Specific – is what I'm delegating too vague?
- Measurable – can I measure the results of what is being delegated?
- Agreed – have we agreed on what needs to be done?
- Realistic – can the person delegated to realistically complete the task? Do they have the resources required to get the job done? Do they have any training needs that I need to consider?
- Timebound – what's the timeframe for completion of the task?
- Ethical – is the task ethical?
- Recorded – have we written down our agreement on the delegated task?

Here is an example of a poorly defined delegated task. **Task: Provide me with the stats on our company's media coverage.** The boss doesn't indicate the time period for the collection of the stats, nor provide a due date for the project. Additionally, specification about which types of media coverage would be helpful.

Successful delegation has a clearly defined beginning, middle, and end.

- Beginning. Remember to provide the context for the task and why you chose the person or team to complete it. What is the task's importance and relevance? Where does it fit in the overall scheme of things? What are they going to get out of it? What am I going to get out of it?

- Middle. Agree upon methods of checking in and updating together. Failing to agree to this in advance will cause your monitoring to seem like interference or lack of trust. And think about who else needs to know about what is going on and how to inform them.

- End. Determine how everyone knows when the job is successfully completed. And if it's an ongoing duty, when are the review dates? If the task is complex and has parts or stages, what are the priorities? And don't forget to provide feedback on whether or not the person delegated achieved the required results.

The following helps turn the poorly defined task "get me our media stats" into a SMARTER delegated task.

- Specific: Provide me with an analysis of our media coverage for our product launch in Q1 through Q2. I want key takeaways in the document and the raw data in an appendix.

- Measurable: Your report should cover all media sources (online, offline, and events).

- Achievable: Check in with me when you have a rough draft so we can determine if you are on the right track and/or if I have any inputs at that point. (As the manager, you also should determine if the staffer has the skill set to complete this task.)

- Relevant: This media analysis of the product launch is part of our overall analysis of media for our business line that I'll ask you to lead next quarter.

- Time-bound: Start this tomorrow and complete it before the end of the week. If you have any issues with making that deadline, let me know ahead of time.

- Ethical: Collect data from verifiable sources and all data analysis should be original. Credit others in your report if the analysis builds on the work of others.
- Recorded: Defined in writing, using this checklist, after both agree to this project being the staffer's responsibility.

Levels of Delegation

Delegation isn't one size fits all. How much autonomy are you delegating? The freedom you delegate to someone for a specific task can run a spectrum from zero (no autonomy) to a hundred (complete autonomy). I have found the Delegated Autonomy Spectrum in Figure 13.1 a helpful tool for managers because it eliminates surprises around scope and decision-making independence down the road.

Adam Learns to Delegate Better I was hired to coach Adam, who was recently promoted to head of brand strategy at a gaming company, because his team had started to complain about the lack of clear priorities and the last-minute crises that accompanied all their major campaigns. Everyone, including Adam, wanted to work with less last-minute stress, but he wasn't sure how to achieve this. Adam had received an adult diagnosis of ADHD earlier in his career, but had never shared it with any of his employers.

0	50	100
None: "Follow these instructions precisely."	**Some:** "Give me your analysis and recommendation, and I'll let you know if you can move ahead."	**Complete:** "Decide and take action, and let me know when it's completed."

Figure 13.1 Delegated Autonomy Spectrum.

I started by having conversations with Adam's team, which helped us establish his three coaching goals: 1) better strategic direction for the team from him, 2) project prioritization, and 3) clarity about people's roles and responsibilities on these projects.

Adam admitted his ADHD was becoming harder to cope with as his responsibilities multiplied. He realized he needed to delegate more to free up some of his time to focus on upcoming campaign strategies, rather than staying in the weeds of project execution.

Adam struggled to keep on top of the planning work for the team, and he agreed to get help from one of his team members, who excelled at project management. This was a step in the right direction. At the same time, Adam was a perfectionist and loved doing the work himself. The SMARTER checklist became a key tool for him. He used it to delegate better, and as a personal checklist for his own work tasks.

Finally, after we walked through the levels of autonomy he could delegate with tasks, Adam had an ah-ha! moment. He realized that identifying and clearly communicating how much autonomy he was delegating with a task helped everyone clarify their roles and responsibilities, and allowed better accountability for results.

I put the SMARTER checklist on my white board and drew the Delegated Autonomy Spectrum up there too, as reminders that I have tools to delegate and communicate better. And, yes, I got feedback from the team that their stress levels were improving.

Key 3: Give Frequent Feedback

Feedback is part of a boss's job.[4] I want to focus here on how to develop your own style for delivering feedback since we covered the basics of delivering it in Chapter 11. Your style comes from knowing your tendencies and practice, practice, practice. . . .

Feedback Is an Act of Love

This is worth repeating. Try to de-emphasize the negative associations of feedback in your mind. If you deliver it neutrally—not with hostility, not apologetically—you help the other person see this as a natural process. Additionally, feedback is an act of love because you are helping someone understand how their actions impact others, something we often are unaware of.

For instance, Gabriela's new puppy needed potty training in the morning, and she ended up doing this during her remote team's morning huddles. Excellent multitasking, but it created a chaotic experience for the rest of the team. Her boss gave her this feedback, and Gabriela was so apologetic. She didn't realize how her distraction impacted the team. Puppy training was rescheduled to earlier in the day—a beautiful example of snack-sized feedback.

Awareness of Your Soft or Tough Tendency[5]

In Chapter 9, we talked about developing awareness of whether you tend to enter into crucial conversations with a tough or soft stance. Can you also bring that awareness to how you deliver feedback? Try leaning into whichever stance you don't automatically favor.

A soft or tough tendency often plays into whether you deliver feedback directly or beat around the bush and have a staffer walk away scratching their head wondering if they did something right or wrong. . . . You want to ensure the person receiving the feedback understands your message. A quick hack to overcome this challenge is to ask the person to summarize your feedback and the agreed upon next steps.

Practice

Feedback is like a muscle that needs to be developed. If you practice giving feedback, you will improve. And one day, it may even become a habit. Challenge yourself to move out of your comfort zone and take some risks. You may not get it right on your first attempts, but you will improve. Start with the following Feedback Challenge for a few weeks and see if delivering positive feedback gets any easier for you, and if it then makes it easier to deliver constructive feedback. It's a beautiful first step.

Feedback on Your Feedback

Critically important, find a way to evaluate how your feedback is landing. I suggest letting your team know you are prioritizing feedback—both delivering it and receiving it. This sets the context for when they see you behave differently. Your one-on-ones are a good opportunity to probe for feedback. This is a safe place for learning. Asking specific questions is important too because vague answers won't help you to improve. "You know I've been trying to deliver more consistent, timely feedback. . . .

- "Have you noticed a difference?"
- "What is working and what needs more improvement?"
- "What feedback and advice do you have for me?"

And don't forget to thank the person for their feedback, no matter how it is delivered.

The Feedback Challenge

- Start with positive feedback and deliver it to everyone on your team at least three times a week for the next month.
- Keep track with a Post-it Notes on your screen, or a note on your phone.

- Each time you deliver positive feedback, note what it felt like for you and the types of reactions you received from your team members.
- After month one, build on this momentum and start delivering "snacks" of constructive feedback. Start small and build in your own feedback loop.

Key 4: Develop Staff Potential through Performance and Career Coaching[6]

Bosses should aim to coach their direct reports both on how they perform their job and what career development looks like for them. Yes, stakes have been raised. The expectation now is that a boss takes an interest in her direct report's career progression and it's an ongoing process, not just a conversation once a year.

Performance Coaching

A boss acts like a coach when they listen actively and provide regular feedback to their direct reports. To take performance coaching a step further, a boss helps their direct reports develop their own problem-solving skills. I recommend David Rock's book *Quiet Leadership: Six Steps to Transforming Performance at Work* to everyone I coach. In essence, adults learn best when they discover their own solutions rather than being told what to do. The boss needs to invest time in this coaching process and the payoff is a more motivated employee, and deeper learning that they own and draw upon in future situations.

Performance coaching rests on the boss helping the staff person to develop different perspectives about a challenge. For performance coaching, there are three steps.

1. Ask questions. The first step is to explore the current situation with questions. I also use numeric scales to help focus the conversation and open up space to explore the WHY behind the number. I prefer a 1 to 4 scale that you adapt to the question: 1, not important; 2, somewhat important; 3, important; 4, urgent.

- **How important is it to you to resolve this issue?**
- **How much thought have you given this issue to date?**
- **What are your main insights about this issue?**

2. Explore options. The second step is to explore options to resolve the issue.

- **How do your insights help make progress on this issue?**
- **What are some options you would consider to move things forward?**

3. Plan next steps and explore motivation. The third step is to focus on the tangible next steps that are built from the options and tap into the person's energy.

- **What is the specific action that you will take?**
- **When do you plan to complete this action?**
- **How can I best help you think through how to move this forward?**

In summary, the boss, as coach, starts the conversation with their direct report by identifying the person's thinking about the issue, then explores options for action, and finally agrees on next steps via tapping into the person's motivations. The boss as coach will want to follow up on the learnings to see what stuck.

Sales Improvements at a Fintech Firm   CEO Mateo was under a lot of pressure from his investors to convert pipeline leads into sales at his fintech firm. He was frustrated with the progress of his new sales lead, Aimee, but wanted her to own the strategies rather than him dictating them to her.

Mateo started by asking Aimee to explain the sales team's strategies, key challenges, and any insights she had developed. She zeroed in on the inexperience of much of the sales team.

Next, Mateo asked Aimee how she could build on her insights to make sales conversions. Aimee wanted to match the inexperienced team members up with more experienced sales people who understood the nuances of pitching to clients.

Mateo agreed with investing in this mentor-apprenticeship training model. He then asked her specific questions about the timeline and actions she was planning.

When Aimee reported back four weeks later, the conversation rate of pipeline leads was up 15%, Mateo commented, Amy was jazzed by the sales progress, and she appreciated my support in helping her tap into her own insights, which she developed into a viable strategy."

Career Coaching

Ten years ago, bosses didn't have the same responsibility for coaching their staff about their careers. Some did; some didn't, and it was more of a choice. Not so today. While not all bosses are naturals at having career development conversations, everyone can become proficient. In *Radical Candor*, Kim Scott describes a three-part conversation (Table 13.2) that all managers should have with direct reports focused on their career dreams and how to achieve them.[7]

These conversations ideally occur within a six-week period. As a guideline, schedule 45 minutes for each of them. The outcomes of these three conversations naturally integrate into regular one-on-one check-ins, and the person's annual development plan, which is required by most employers in some format or another.

Claudia Clarifies Her Dream Claudia had been at a Fortune 100 financial services company for over a decade helping manage agile teams that worked on big data projects. She had an excellent track record helping new teams get set up for success and crush their goals. Claudia was a SVP and from the outside, everything

Table 13.2 Three-Part Career Coaching Conversation.

Conversation 1: Story of You	Conversation 2: Dreams, Aspirations	Conversation 3: 18-Month Plan
Goal: Understand what motivates the person, including what they care about and value	Goal: Understand the person's dreams and aspirations	Goal: Translate current work to future dreams through a learning agenda
A get-to-know-you-conversation • Tell me about your life. • What changes have you made in your life and what drove those choices? • What motivates you?	A dreams and values alignment conversation • What do you dream about doing at work? In your career? In life? (Ask for 3–5 dreams for the future.) • What does success look like to you? • What would a good life look like to you? In 5–10 years? • Do these dreams align with the values you expressed in our first conversation?	They should ask themselves: • How do I prioritize my dreams? • What do I need to learn to move toward my dreams? • How should I prioritize the things I need to learn? • Whom can I learn from? When someone is clear on what they want to learn, it's easier for a boss to find opportunities for them to develop the skills identified over the next 6–18 months.

(Continued)

Table 13.2   (Continued)

Conversation 1: Story of You	Conversation 2: Dreams, Aspirations	Conversation 3: 18-Month Plan
Output: Both people keep notes to record the conversation and for reflection.	Output: A chart with the 3–5 dreams in columns and the skills needed to achieve each dream listed in the rows. This gets the person starting to think about skills they want to build to achieve their dreams. It may also help them prioritize their aspirations.	Output: An action plan. List options of how this person's role can change to help them learn skills to achieve their dreams; whom they can learn from; courses and books to explore, etc. Each of these action items needs clarity on who does what, by when. It becomes a simple and highly effective accountability tool.

Source: Adapted from Chapter 7, *Radical Candor* by Kim Scott, 2017.

looked great, but she wasn't feeling motivated about her career. When a new boss arrived, their conversation made Claudia re-examine her goals. The new boss used a process similar to the three-part career conversation outlined in Table 13.2, and it helped Claudia clarify her dream to launch her own consulting firm rather than work toward a managing director promotion. Together they mapped out how Claudia would get as much relevant experience as possible over the next one to two years to help her make a smooth transition. In fact, Claudia was able to build her side-hustle, with full support of her boss, and in 18 months, she had started her business, and her old employer became one of her first clients.

In Claudia's words: "I needed the support and perspective of my new boss to own my dream, and to have the permission to realize that becoming a managing director wasn't what motivated me. I am a born trainer and consultant, and I'm good at it. I'm thrilled that I was nudged to own what I really wanted to do, and to activate the steps to make it happen."

The Management Building Block Challenge

- Rate yourself on a scale of 1 to 4 on each of the four keys to great management. (1 = poor; 2 = okay for now; 3 = good; 4 = excellent). (You also could do this exercise with a couple of trusted colleagues to get a sense of others' perceptions of your management skills.)
- Write down a couple of sentences explaining why you gave yourself the score that you did for each of the four keys.
- Select your lowest score and brainstorm two or three actions you could take to improve that score.
- Commit to one of these actions and put a couple of check-ins on your calendar to monitor your progress in changing your behavior.

Resources

- Manager Tools, the podcast and online platform, is your go-to for basic management tools. The platform covers in depth these four basics of management. It also outlines a roll-out plan for introducing the different elements of this framework to your team. The founders of Manager Tools are both ex-military, and I deeply appreciate their direct, unfussy communication style. https://www.manager-tools.com/manager-tools-basics

- *The Coaching Habit: Say Less, Ask More and Change the Way You Lead Forever* by Michael Bungay-Stanier, Page Two Books (2016). So much of Michael's book is about helping bosses to ask the right questions when they coach their staff. He lays it out in a highly practical and actionable way.

- *Radical Candor* by Kim Scott, St. Martin's Publishing (2017). Chapter 7, "Getting Results with Effective Collaboration" is devoted entirely to career coaching conversations between managers and direct reports. And the key word here is *conversation*.

- *Quiet Leadership* by David Rock (2006) is an evergreen resource for bosses to consider about how to help their direct reports learn to problem solve for themselves. It all starts with powerful coaching questions!

14

GRPI: A Diagnostic Framework to Unlock Team Needs

A correct diagnosis is three-fourths the remedy.

—Mahatma Gandhi

GRPI stands for Goals, Roles and Responsibilities, Processes, and Interpersonal Relationships. These concepts may seem so basic that we would expect bosses to understand them without needing a framework! But in my experience, GRPI has proven to be a helpful diagnostic tool for many managers confronted with workplace challenges.

A savvy, trusted colleague, Michelle, introduced me to GRPI, a 50-year-old framework put forth by organizational theorist Richard Beckhard in 1972, and I started using it immediately in my coaching practice because I saw how powerful it was as a diagnostic tool.[1] Bosses can use it as a checklist to understand the root of a work problem. Problems at the top of the hierarchy cascade down if they aren't resolved. GRPI helps diagnose the actual problem and where it resides in this hierarchy because responses and solutions are not one size fits all.

Of course, life is more complicated than this. Often a problem in the workplace has multiple dimensions, making it hard to pinpoint the original cause but digging down to understand the core of the problem is extremely valuable. I have seen bosses who initially assumed interpersonal issues were at the heart of a workplace challenge use GRPI to discover that unclear goals, roles, or processes were the true pain point. As boss, employing GRPI demonstrates you show up ready to do the work and get to the heart of the issue, rather than stick with the most obvious read of the situation.

I worked with an international pharma company, and the CFO believed leaders of the corporate finance team had personality clashes with the finance leads of the international divisions. We used GRPI as a diagnostic tool and discovered that the real essence of the dysfunction was that goals and incentive structures were not aligned. Once he focused here, progress occurred. In his words, "All I could see was how badly these finance leaders treated each other. I fell into the trap of assuming it was about personalities when we actually had other issues to attend to first."

The GRPI Hierarchy

GRPI is an acronym describing the different dimensions characterizing a team. GRPI is intended to be used as a hierarchy, as Table 14.1 shows.

Ambiguity at one level cascades down and has an impact on the next level, and problems on a lower level are often symptoms of conflicts on a higher level.

- If goals are unclear, uncertainties in roles and responsibilities arise.
- If roles are unclear, conflict in processes (how to work together) emerge.
- If processes are unclear, conflict emerges in interpersonal relationships.

Table 14.1 GRPI at a Glance.[2]

G **Goals**: Clarity about the team's purpose and priorities.
- Foundation of good teamwork.
- Defines where the team is now and where it wants to go.
- Creates a sense of identity.
- Majority of team conflicts are attributed to unclear goals.

R **Roles and Responsibilities**: Clarity about who does what and scope of their work.
- Roles support the defined goals.
- Clarity about authority, responsibility, and tasks is required.
- Individual and collective accountability is required.

P **Processes and Procedures**: Clarity about how the team accomplishes its work.
- Specifically: norms, decision making, communication, conflict management, coordination, resource allocation, planning, etc.
- Processes are needed to overcome team inefficiencies.
- Processes effectively support the team's goals by determining the interactions within a team.

I **Interpersonal Relationships**: Clarity that team members' relationships are healthy and support the team's work.
- Establishment of high trust, open communication, feedback between team members.
- Specific norms have to be established, understood, and agreed upon.

Clear goal setting is obvious but neglected so frequently. Having clear goals articulated and written down before a team is launched is fundamental to success. And remember to revisit those goals and revise them in writing if they change along the way. My **quick hack** is that every team member, if asked, should be able to articulate the team's goals without any hesitation. Likewise, a team needs to identify any issues that limit it from reaching its goals and addressing issues that may be roadblocks to accomplishing goals.

Beatriz Uses GRPI to Understand a Leadership Team's Challenge My client Beatriz was responsible for a major refugee relief project in Eastern Africa. Her senior leadership team included several department heads: programs, operations, security, finance, and human resources. She had excellent relationships with each of them, but felt they worked too independently of each other, and weren't collaborating enough to solve cross-reaching problems such as coordinating emergency service delivery with local partners, while ensuring the safety of the organization's field staff. She had concluded that this lack of collaboration was rooted in interpersonal conflict between these team members. We used the GRPI framework to do a more accurate diagnosis of the situation. She quickly confirmed the team was very clear on goals, and their roles and responsibilities. However, Beatriz realized that problems showing up as interpersonal conflict were actually due to poor communication between the various departments. She had regular one-on-ones with the department heads, but realized two process issues needed to be addressed:

- Decisions made one-on-one with her weren't being communicated to other department heads in a timely manner.
- Department heads needed to problem solve together without relying on her so heavily.

Based on these insights, Beatriz made the following changes:

- At their regular leadership team meetings, time was set aside to ensure all recent decisions were presented and captured in the minutes. This helped on the communication front.
- Beatriz clarified to the team that before she'd sign off on a department head's recommendation, she'd need assurance it had received buy-in from other departments affected by the decision. For instance, when the programs team wanted to prioritize the opening of new health clinics over employment training programs, Beatriz approved the recommendation only once she was certain the other department heads agreed with the proposal.

- She asked the leadership team to organize quarterly meetings without her where they worked through thorny issues as a team, and then brought them to her. The department heads each took turns running these meetings.

As Beatriz explained: "It seemed so obvious to me that different personalities were clashing and causing tensions across the leadership team. But GRPI was invaluable in getting to the root of the problem. And it's not lost on me that I also had to change my behavior as a leader. To be honest, I was concerned that getting the department heads to coordinate more before bringing a proposal to me would slow things down. On the contrary, yes, it took a little longer for a proposal to get to me, but then execution was much smoother because we had buy-in, and that ultimately saved us a lot of time."

Coaches are often called in when interpersonal conflict has become problematic. I have learned that if we focus our efforts there, we may be missing the real issues that need resolving. This framework helps us to articulate the right open-ended questions to determine where the problem resides.

Reflection Questions

- Is my team clear about its goals? Can everyone articulate them clearly?
- Are we all clear how our roles and responsibilities contribute to achieving our team's goals? Where are the synergies and points of tension here?
- Do we have ways of communicating, making decisions, and resolving conflict that help us do our jobs and achieve our goals?
- Are we looking at interpersonal conflict within the bigger framework of GRPI?

Resources

- *The GRPI Model – An Approach for Team Development* by Steve Raue, Suk-Han Tang, Christian Weiland, and Claas Wenzlik (2013), Version 2, Systemic Excellence Group, Independent Think Tank for Leading Practice. This is an academic dive into GRPI; it goes into detail about using it as a team-building tool, not just as a diagnostic one.
- "A Model for the Executive Management of Transformational Change", Chapter 7, by Richard Beckhard in *The Pfeiffer Book of Successful Leadership Development Tools, 1st Edition*, Jack Gordon, Editor (2007).

15

Six Keys to Unlock the Power of a Strong Team

Start by doing what's necessary, then what's possible, and suddenly you are doing the impossible

— St. Francis of Assisi

What does it take to have a successful team? This is the topic of countless business books, courses, and keynote presentations. Building a successful team is challenging and complicated. It is rarely easy. At the same time, a general purpose framework describing the building blocks of a successful team is a valuable way to focus team members on success and create team norms. Six Keys to Building a Strong Team is the framework I use most extensively working with teams. I drew heavy inspiration from Patrick Lencioni's bestselling book *The Five Behaviors of a Dysfunctional Team: A Leadership Fable.* I pay homage to him and his pioneering work in helping us look at team cohesion from a practical, layered perspective.

I chose the word *strong* intentionally because a strong team is capable, energetic, tenacious, and implies collective focus on achieving goals, whether that is social change, a technology breakthrough, or revenue targets. The value of becoming a strong team is that the team will function at a higher level, with less stress and more cooperation. Projects will run more smoothly, and team members will be happier at work.

This is a highly flexible framework. It can be used equally for understanding the dynamics of a leadership team as it can for a short-term ad hoc project team. I use it to enter into a conversation with a team about what is working and what can be improved. Time and time again in my work with teams, I am reminded that we all want to enjoy work, we want it to be satisfying and stimulating, and we want to feel like respected members of our teams. Those are basic building blocks for thriving at work and delivering results.

A very practical way to use this framework is to have the team self-diagnose which of the six keys in Figure 15.1 are most challenging for the team, and then focus on changing awareness

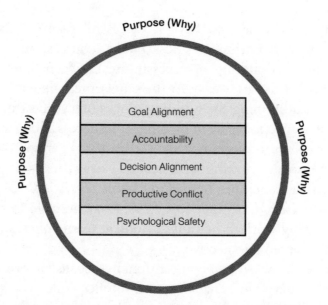

Figure 15.1   Six Keys to Unlock the Power of a Strong Team.

and behaviors there. These layers are individual building blocks that complete the whole. I always start at the bottom building block since psychological safety underpins everything.

Psychological Safety

At the individual level it means to "show and employ one's self without fear of negative consequences of self-image, status, or career." (See Table 15.1.) At the team level, it means "a shared belief held by members of a team that the team is safe for interpersonal risks."[1] In other words, we feel safe in our team to show up as whole people, to express opinions, take risks, and fess up to mistakes without fear of consequences to our reputations or our careers.[2]

Table 15.1 Psychological Safety.

When the team embodies psychological safety	How to build psychological safety	Reflection questions
▪ Members feel accepted and respected by others. ▪ Members are comfortable sharing mistakes and fears. ▪ They ask for help. ▪ Team benefits from more engagement and creativity in problem solving and project collaboration. ▪ Members let go of grudges, offer and accept apologies.	▪ Learn each other's work and communication styles (e.g., DiSC). ▪ Spend time socializing together. ▪ For leaders, speak out less and focus on how you react and respond to team members. ▪ For leaders, ensure gossip is not tolerated.	▪ How can you learn about each other's working style and use that information to build trust? ▪ How often do you admit mistakes and weaknesses on this team? ▪ Do you accept questions about your area of responsibility? ▪ Do you readily offer and accept apologies?

A New Law School Chair Starts to Build Psychological Safety Sheila was recently promoted to head of admissions at an Ivy League law school. The leadership team she inherited was having trouble adjusting to her style, which was very different from her predecessor. Sheila knew a couple of members of the team had not supported her promotion. She also knew she needed to demonstrate that everyone on the leadership team was safe, and had a voice in the department's management.

As a way to ease into discussing psychological safety, at their first offsite, I asked the group to answer the following three questions[3]:

1. Where were you born?
2. Where are you in the birth order of your family?
3. What was your biggest challenge as a child?

Sheila started and shared that she was born in Atlanta, was the oldest of three daughters, and her biggest challenge growing up was that her father was killed by a drunk driver when she was 11 years old. No one on the team, even though some had been her colleagues for years, knew about this tragedy. Her vulnerability opened the way for others to share about their challenges, including one woman who recounted her family's story as refugees to the USA. Sheila realized psychological safety builds up over time, but she felt confident that sharing their challenges and vulnerabilities so readily was a key first step for this team, and she was committed to continuing the journey with them.

Productive Conflict

A team engages in passionate, maybe even heated, discussion about ideas and options because it knows it's the fastest way to making good decisions. Team members don't hesitate to question

Table 15.2 Productive Conflict.

When the team embodies productive conflict	How to build productive conflict	Reflection questions
• Conflict is helpful to advance work, and make faster, efficient decisions. • Conflict is about ideas not people. • Team members are more engaged and feel they have a voice on important issues. • Meetings aren't boring.	• Establish team norms around acceptable conflict behaviors, e.g., raised voices, profanities, being emotional, and/or going beyond the meeting end time to resolve a conflict. • For leaders, positively reinforce productive team norms, and quickly react to unproductive behavior.	• Are our behaviors productive or unproductive when facing conflict? • What can we do to ensure those less comfortable with conflict have a voice? • When conflict occurs, does the team confront and deal with the issue before moving on?

or challenge each other to get the best answers. This (along with accountability) is usually the most challenging for teams. For more on productive conflict, see Table 15.2.

Productive Conflict in Staff Meetings Can Be a Good Thing   My friend Luis is head of production for a successful, well-known podcaster. The podcast team of eight (podcast host, production team, marketing team, and the content team) has a weekly staff meeting. I know Luis hates to miss them. I was intrigued because I'd heard him say they lasted up to three hours. Personally, I found the idea of a three-hour staff meeting horrifying. But he explained they are fun because they always end up in friendly arguments about guests, topics for future episodes, and even what kinds of questions the host should ask. Everyone has to participate; that's a rule. Luis said that he feels free to disagree and challenge colleagues about their perspectives, even the famous podcast host! In his words, "It is liberating and the time flies." He also loves the fact that they get a lot of decisions made in these meetings because "nothing is left unsaid" so decisions happen more quickly.

Decision Alignment

A team achieves buy-in on important decisions. This is not decision by consensus. Buy-in occurs because everyone has the opportunity to weigh in and share opinions and ideas. Not every team member may agree with the final decision, but everyone needs to fully support it and walk out of the meeting as a united front. For more on decision alignment, see Table 15.3.

Table 15.3 Decision Alignment.

When the team embodies decision alignment	How to build decision alignment	Reflection questions
• Team members are confident their opinions are heard. • No time is wasted revisiting decisions that were made without full team input. • The team is a united front once the decision is made. • Each team member can clearly explain the team's decision and next steps to others.	• Build decision alignment through trust and productive conflict at the team level. • Ensure the process leading to a team decision includes opportunities for everyone to participate, debate, and share perspectives.	• Is the team clear about its overall direction and priorities? • How do matrix issues affect decision alignment? • How do you ensure all team members are committed to a decision when they walk out of a meeting, even if it wasn't the decision they wanted to see made?

Accountability

Team members hold each other accountable for getting the work done and for behaving according to agreed-upon team norms. Accountability (along with productive conflict) is usually the most challenging for teams to embrace. For more on accountability, see Table 15.4.

Time and again, I have seen the power of what happens when team members hold each other accountable. I recently sat in on a quarterly review meeting of a leadership team I coach. This was a team I'd worked with for several months. At the meeting, I heard them call each other out for interrupting and talking over each other. I also heard them ask each other tough questions about missed revenue targets and product delays. I later asked

Table 15.4 Accountability.

When the team embodies accountability	How to build accountability	Reflection questions
▪ Everyone knows the team lead will hold everyone accountable, and at the same time, expects them to hold each other accountable. ▪ Everyone recognizes that individual feedback benefits the team as a whole. ▪ People expect others to ask questions about their area of responsibility and welcome their inputs	▪ Train and mentor team members in how to give feedback. ▪ Ensure team members have regular 1:1 check-ins. ▪ Review progress against goals during team meetings, and address missed deadlines ASAP. ▪ For leaders, deliver feedback consistently (lead by example).	▪ Do team members deliver positive feedback to each other? ▪ Do team members offer constructive feedback to each other? ▪ Do team members feel comfortable questioning each other about their strategies and methods?

one of them to explain what had changed. He said ". . . having clear, agreed upon team norms was a key step. And we have been practicing these accountability behaviors for a while . . . it feels good to see that we are finally hitting our stride."

Goal Alignment

Team members align on team goals, rather than focusing on their individual goals and career plans. Team and individual success is achieved through team goals. For more on goal alignment, see Table 15.5.

Table 15.5 Goal Alignment.

When the team focuses on common results	How to build focus on common results	Reflection questions
• Team members don't place their career or ego ahead of the results that define team success. • Team members avoid distractions. • Collective results are valued over individual results.	• Ensure the performance review system is centered on team goals, rather than individual ones; and compensation and bonuses are linked in part to team performance. • For leaders, ensure processes and structures help your team to focus on common goals.	• Do members value team success more than individual success? • Will team members make sacrifices for the good of the team? • Do team members recognize the contributions of others in achieving team goals? • When the team doesn't achieve its collective goals, does everyone take ownership for making improvements?

*A **Fashion Company's Long-Term Growth Comes at a Cost*** I have a long-standing corporate client that is shifting direction away from operating its own retail outlets to selling its fashion accessories wholesale. The retail outlets are generating a lot of the funds to support the growth of the wholesale business. This strong team framework requires everyone on the leadership team to be focused on the same common results. The work that went into developing this goal alignment across departments was a big lift, but critically important for the company's longer-term prospects.

Purpose

A team is aligned on the meaning of its work and has a vision of what it wants to build and achieve. Purpose taps into both individual and team motivation. For more on purpose, see Table 15.6.

Table 15.6 Purpose (The "Why" Behind the Work).

When the team embodies purpose	How to build purpose	Reflection questions
<ul><li>The team has a North Star to guide it through challenges.</li><li>Decisions are made more easily because the team is clear about the "why" behind its work.</li><li>Team members are more motivated and experience greater meaning through their work.</li></ul>	<ul><li>Invest time in developing team values, and a team mission and vision.</li><li>Create rituals and routines that validate the team's purpose, e.g., celebrate when important goals are met.</li><li>For leaders, use staff surveys to gauge team clarity of purpose.</li></ul>	<ul><li>What is your team's North Star?</li><li>What motivates individual team members?</li><li>Can the team define a collective motivation?</li><li>Can the team define the "why" driving its work?</li></ul>

Nonprofit Changes Focus and Maintains Its Purpose   I am lucky enough to serve on a nonprofit board that helps low-income women develop the skills needed to find employment in the food industry. The organization started out as a business, and then later transitioned into a more traditional workforce development nonprofit. Razor-clear purpose allowed it to successfully shift direction, and enabled the board, leadership, and staff to weather these significant changes.

Reflection Questions

- Where is our team strongest (i.e., which of the six keys?), and how can we leverage that strength better?
- Where does our team need to improve most? And how do we articulate those team improvement goals?
- What are the concrete next steps to achieve those goals and how will we measure success?

Resources

- *The Five Dysfunctions of a Team: A Leadership Fable* (2002) and *The Advantage* (2012) by Patrick Lencioni, Jossey-Bass, are excellent books if you want a grounding in how to achieve team success. The first is written like a novel and very accessible. *The Advantage* builds the first book and emphasizes how leadership teams need to build strong internal communication processes.
- *The Fearless Organization: Creating Psychological Safety in the Workplace for Learning, Innovation and Growth* by Amy Edmondson, Wiley (2018). This book explores the culture of psychological safety and why you need it if your organization is committed to constant learning and healthy innovation.

- "What Google Learned From Its Quest to Build the Perfect Team" by Charles Duhigg, The *New York Times Magazine*, February 28, 2016. This is an evergreen article that outlines the five key learnings of what makes a successful team. Hint: the most important is psychological safety.
- "Simon Sinek: How Great Leaders Inspire Action" | *TED Talk* (2009). This went viral and hit a nerve—what is the WHY behind what companies do? This is TED's third most popular TED Video of all time. The TED Talk is based on Simon's book *Start with Why: How Great Leaders Inspire Everyone to Take Action* (2009).

V

Crossing the Finish Line and Solidifying Your Coaching Wins

We focus on making your coaching wins stick in Part V. You have worked hard to achieve change, how do you now maintain it? I present two proven strategies: habit formation in Chapter 16, and RAM-3, 2, 1—a mnemonic I developed to avoid backtracking on your coaching wins—in Chapter 17.

I want to stress this is not a separate process from the coaching work. You are doing both simultaneously: developing your awareness and changing behavior, *and* building ways to maintain your coaching wins. Luckily, these suggestions are just as viable whether you have your own coach or are coaching yourself with this book as your guide.

16

Building Powerful Habits

We are what we repeatedly do. Excellence, then, is not an act, but a habit.
—Aristotle

There is an abundance of literature and research about the neuroscience of habits and the building blocks to sustain good habits. What can I say in a few pages about habits when so many excellent books have already been written? I start with a focus on the work of three well-known authors, Charles Duhigg, BJ Fogg, and James Clear, because I find their work to be the most instructive and relatable when it comes to identifying, developing, and maintaining habits.

Charles Duhigg first published *The Power of Habit* in 2012 and explained in simple language why habits are core to everything we do and how to change them. He popularized the term *habit loop* and also coined the term *keystone habits* — foundational habits that ripple positively into other parts of our life. His core message is that the most effective way to shift a habit is to diagnose and retain the habit "cue" and "reward" and try to change only the "routine." For instance, I feel low energy in the afternoon (cue) and change my routine from buying a chocolate chip cookie to walking around and having a chat with a colleague. And my reward remains the same: I stretch my legs and re-energize my mood.

James Clear hit a nerve when *Atomic Habits* was published in 2018. He helped us see how habits are closely linked to the kind of person we want to be. He also emphasized that small incremental changes can compound into remarkable results. And he preaches that good habits are easier to achieve when you make them obvious, attractive, easy, and satisfying. For instance, I find it easier to save money if I have an obvious and attractive goal like saving for a vacation. I made this new habit easier by setting up a direct transfer into my savings account each month. And I find it satisfying to see this vacation fund growing month by month.

The essence of BJ Fogg's *Tiny Habits* (2020) is to take a behavior you want, make it tiny, find where it fits naturally in your life, and nurture its growth. We already have numerous habits we engage in daily, and we can use them as anchors to start new habits. As well, we need to remember to celebrate our tiny habits as they develop into solid, bigger habits. For instance, to positively transition into my evening after I turn off my computer monitor at the end of the workday (**anchor**), I recall an accomplishment (**tiny habit**), and then say out loud, "nice job, Antonia" (**celebrate**).

Writing this chapter reinforced to me that successful habit formation is *highly* personal. We need to consider the development of positive, strong habits as a journey rather than a destination. It is your journey, and approaching it with a learning mindset will make it less stressful and more joyful.

Who Do You Want to Be?
(Intentions, Goals, and Habits)

For me, the key truth about forming good habits starts by answering the question: Who do you want to be? You have been addressing this question throughout your coaching journey. And, yes, it is a broad question! Determine the right intentions for yourself, and they become the North Star for your coaching work, and ultimately, the habits you form to help you get there. What is my intention?

- Do I want to be a loving, empathetic partner to my partner?
- Do I want to be a motivating boss for my team?
- Do I want to be a peak fitness performer for myself?

For example, if I have the intention to achieve peak fitness, I may set the goal of running a half marathon. And that goal is hard to achieve without developing the habit of a regular training schedule.

Habits ladder up to achieve your goals, which in turn, are linked to your broader intentions. See the continuum? The key takeaway is that intentions aren't enough to change behavior, they need to cascade down into goals and strong habits help you achieve your goals.

Question Cascade
- What are my **intentions** at work? at home? for myself?
- What are the **goals** linked to my intentions?
- And which positive **habits** do I need to develop to achieve my goals?

Habit Basics

Research tells us that 40% of the actions people perform every day aren't due to decision making but to habits.[1] Habits are behaviors you have repeated so many times they have become more or less automatic. Habits can have different implications: positive (eating vegetables daily), negative (binging Netflix for hours on end while eating potato chips), or neutral (knowing how to work a dishwasher). We need these automatic shortcuts to help manage and process all the information and stimuli bombarding us every day. And when we can successfully automate positive, healthy, new skills, our brain can focus on learning other healthy skills, solving problems, and pursuing creative projects.[2]

The Habit Loop

This term has entered our common lexicon because habits have generated enormous interest in recent years. It originates in research done at MIT in the 1990s.[3] Simply put, a habit loop is when something triggers you to have a thought or perform an action, and that thought or action delivers you a reward, so you keep doing it. The tricky part is a habit loop can occur without us even realizing it.

Charles Duhigg's work emphasizes a three-part loop: cue, routine, reward. And he focuses on changing the routine, while keeping the cue and reward the same, to develop better habits.

James Clear expanded the habit loop to have four parts: cue, craving, routine, reward. His addition of craving acknowledges the important role of motivation in habit formation. A craving is about wanting to change your internal state in some way. For instance, I don't brush my teeth because I enjoy it, but because I want the satisfaction of seeing my white teeth reflected back in the mirror. My cousin has yellow, stained teeth and doesn't care. He considers tooth brushing an optional activity. Different people have different motivations.

Taking the time to develop a sound understanding of how habits work will help you build better new habits. I want everyone who reads this chapter to walk away with this mantra in their mind: "Willpower won't get me there, but changing my processes will."

Table 16.1 shows James Clear's four-part habit framework.

Table 16.1   How Does a Habit Loop Work?

Cue ⟶	Craving ⟶	Routine ⟶	Reward
A **cue** is an internal or external stimulus that initiates a behavior. A cue is a small piece of information that tells our brain a reward is close at hand, and leads to a craving.	A **craving** is the motivation behind a habit. A craving results from how you interpret a cue based on your feelings, thoughts or emotions. What you crave is not the habit itself, but the change in state it delivers.	A **routine** is an action. It is the behavior you wish to change (e.g., smoking or biting your nails) or build (e.g., taking the stairs instead of the elevator).	A **reward** is the benefit you gain from doing the habit. A reward can be immediate and/or longer-term. A reward is the reason the brain decides the previous steps are worth remembering for the future.

A couple of examples bring this theory to life.

Cue ⟵	Craving ⟵	Routine ⟵	Reward
You notice your teeth are stained from drinking coffee.	You want whiter teeth.	You rinse your mouth with water immediately after drinking coffee.	You satisfy your craving to have whiter teeth. Rinsing your mouth becomes associated with drinking coffee.
You experience writer's block when working on a report at work.	You feel stuck and want to reduce your frustration.	You take a short stroll outside the office.	You satisfy your craving to feel less frustrated by taking a short stroll. Strolling becomes associated with overcoming writer's block at work.

How to Build a New Habit

As you can see in Figure 16.1, the habit loop is a continuous circle with four points. You can think about developing a new habit from any of the four points in the circle. But typically when building a habit, you start with craving because that is your source of motivation linked to the inner state (feeling) that you are seeking.

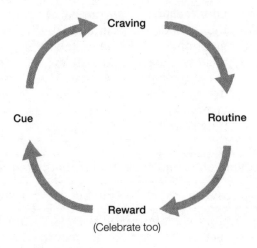

Craving

Routine

Cue

Reward
(Celebrate too)

Figure 16.1   Habit Loop.

How do you put the habit loop into action when you want to build a new habit? The steps below are in a different order than the cue-craving-routine-reward flow in Table 16.1 because there is a difference between *understanding* the concept of the habit loop and how you navigate the loop to *build* a new habit.

Habit Formation: What habit can you create so you start the work week feeling calm and in control?

Step 1: Identify your craving. What motivates you? What feeling are you seeking? You crave the reward, not the routine.

I want to start the week feeling calm and in control with a plan for tackling the week ahead.

Step 2: Identify the routine. The craving motivates a routine you want to become a habit over time. Be as specific as possible about the routine you want to establish.

I will dedicate 30–45 minutes before the week starts to plan my week ahead by reviewing my calendar, upcoming deadlines, and to-do list.

Step 3: Isolate the cue. You want to cue yourself to help build and solidify a new routine. Almost all cues involved in habit formation fit into one of five categories: location, time, emotional state, other people, and the immediately preceding action. You need to get curious about how you can set yourself up for success. What are your current cues and how can they help you to implement your new routine? In our example of developing a habit that allows you to start the work week feeling calm and in control, we landed on the following questions:

- What is a good time to implement your new planning routine?
- Which day is better? Saturday or Sunday?

- Where are you on Sunday night?
- What is your emotional state on Sunday night?
- Which actions precede your new planning routine?

When I finish eating dinner on Sunday night, I set aside 30–45 minutes to create my weekly plan.

Step 4: Identify reward. This is the reward that satisfies your craving.

After planning, I feel positive and calm about the week ahead rather than dreading it.

Celebrate. Remember **to celebrate** the completion of your weekly planning session to send a positive message to yourself and to reinforce the habit loop.[4] A celebration is an immediate reward that can be as small a gesture as saying "good job!" to yourself.

I will let myself watch an episode of my favorite series after I complete my weekly planning.

Key Success Factors for Building Powerful Habits

After exhaustively reviewing the habit literature, here's what I found to be key success factors that all the researchers and writers agree upon.

Start Small

Start small, even ridiculously small. This can mean starting with one push up when you wake up or one minute of meditation. The goal is to make your habit so tiny to start with that you can easily complete it every day without having to rely on willpower. Then you can build tiny habits into bigger habits.[5]

We underestimate the value of making day-to-day incremental improvements even though they pay off in a big way over time. If you saved a dollar a day for 50 years, you'd have $500,000 toward your retirement needs.[6] That's the impact of compound interest. James Clear applies the concept of compounding to habits. If you can get 1% better at a specific behavior each day for a year, you'll end up 37 times better by the time you are done. Conversely, if you get 1% worse each day for one year, you'll decline nearly down to zero.[7]

Environment

Your environment is a key cue that can set you up for success or interfere with positive habit change.

- If you are trying to eat more healthy foods, having healthy foods in your fridge and cupboards, and healthy snacks easily accessible on your countertops are positive environmental cues for eating better. And keep junk food in a top cupboard where it's hard to reach![8]
- In the famous research study on why so many Vietnam vets kicked their heroin habits successfully after returning home, they determined that radical environmental changes played a big role. Coming home meant the soldiers had left behind the environmental cues associated with their heroin use.[9]

Repetition

Changing habits is about repetition. The more you practice, the more success you have.

The Habit of Physical Therapy If you've ever gone to physical therapy (PT) over the course of a few weeks or months, you've probably experienced the cycle of change through repetition. Many people hate PT. It's incremental, it's slow. Perhaps you injured your Achilles tendon and were told by your physician to go to physical therapy for at least three months. You meet with the physical therapist and they tell you to have patience and faith in the process. They promise that you will eventually be back to running and walking as fast as you once did—but with less pain and maybe even at a faster clip. You are dubious. Physical therapy is boring—the therapist has you walking, slowly, on the treadmill, for 15 minutes a session, for several weeks. The routine is tedious; nothing hurts, but it also feels like nothing is happening. You can't see any results at all. Then, one day, the physical therapist says she has good news: Today is the day she is turning up the speed on the treadmill and adding in a hill. You're ready! You step onto the treadmill. The pace is accelerated and you feel the hill come at you. All of a sudden, you find you can run half a mile! Repetition pays off.

Stacking

Stacking is an excellent strategy for building a new habit. Given that unconscious actions account for about 40% of what we do each day, we can leverage an existing habit by adding on to it the new habit we want to introduce. This strategy requires you to take the time to dissect current habits and figure out how to build on top of them.

For instance, I don't like stretching and try to avoid it. At the same time, I want a more flexible, pain-free body. I tried to determine where I could introduce it on top of an existing habit. I change into pajamas every night and I decided to put my roller on top of my pajamas, cueing me to use it when I get ready for bed. I started small too, just 30 seconds of rolling. Over time I built it up to a five-minute stretch/roll routine before bed. And, yes, for many months I would congratulate myself aloud when I finished. "Nice, Antonia . . . your body thanks you."

Reinforcing habits with **positive feedback** works better than negative feedback. Positive feedback satisfies feelings of mastery, effectiveness, and our ability to make good choices, boosting intrinsic motivation. And that's what we are looking for, you being able to motivate yourself. Positive feedback also helps develop long-term motivation, while negative feedback is limited to short-term motivation to avoid an undesirable consequence.[10]

This is why we should **celebrate** our victories along the way and always immediately after doing the new behavior to create positive emotions. For instance, try doing a physical movement like a fist pump to signify victory, or yelling something aloud like "I rock" or "Go, me." You want to get your brain to associate the accomplishment of your habit with feeling good to help turn your new behavior into a habit.

How I Applied the Habit Loop Framework to Improve my Life

I want to share some personal stories of my habit changes over the years because there is no one way to build and change habits. It is deeply personal. It requires **patience** (think 1% improvements); it requires **practice** (repetitions); and it requires a **positive** outlook (a learning mindset) about your ability for change, and specifically change that lasts.

My Water Drinking Habit   I don't like water. It's boring. I know hydration is important, but water doesn't interest me. I exercise a lot and often get dehydrated. For over 10 years I failed at my New Year's resolution to drink more water. I now drink several glasses of water every day, and I have been doing so for over two years. I can safely say I have finally built a solid water-drinking habit. Here is how I built it using the habit loop as my guide.

Craving: I want to be healthy and that includes drinking enough water to flush out toxins and ensure good digestion and circulation.

Cue: I like to drink tea and probably consume several cups a day, so this is a habit I can build on. My cue is turning the kettle on to heat my water for tea. (Note: Figuring out the best cue is critical and might take some experimentation.) This is also a great example of both habit stacking and using my environmental cues to my advantage.

Routine: Research suggests starting with a tiny behavior (e.g., a sip of water) and working your way up to "bigger" behaviors. Every time I turned on the kettle, I went straight to the sink and drank at least two gulps of water while I waited for the water to boil. Gradually, I worked up to this being an entire glass of water.

Reward: I satisfy my craving to be healthier by drinking a glass of water. And drinking the water has become associated with turning on the kettle to make tea.

Celebration: I used to do a fist pump to celebrate each glass of water that I drank and to wire the habit into my brain. I did that for two months. I no longer need to do that because the habit is ingrained.

After a couple of months of this new routine, the strangest thing happened. Not only was I drinking a glass of water every time I waited for the kettle to boil, but I started putting a glass of water on my desk and on my bedside at night (and drinking them). This highlights the value of starting small: I started with a couple of gulps of water when the kettle was boiling and that compounded into drinking water at my desk and in bed! I can't say

I enjoy water more than I used to, but I drink it and don't debate with myself whether or not to drink it like I used to. I just do it.

Smooth Out the Sharp Edges—Intentions Aren't Habits This is something I have been working on for a long time! I can become intense and direct when I feel stressed. Friends, family, and colleagues tell me they experience me as curt and extremely matter of fact in those situations. My first coaching professor and mentor, Joanne Killmeyer, likened my style when stressed to a wooden clapperboard (think "action" and "cut" on a movie set).

Over the years, I tried different approaches to soften my style. I started writing down "smooth out my sharp edges" on Post-it Notes and sticking them on my laptop screen. I journaled about it. I also asked my family to tell me when they experienced it. Yes, I made some progress, but not enough.

When I started delving into habit formation as part of my coaching work a few years ago, I realized that "smooth out my sharp edges" was an intention. And intentions are terrific, but they are not specific enough for behavior change.

I recognized I needed to work on the small behavioral goals that help me to smooth out my edges. I doubled down on understanding who I wanted to be: a patient, empathetic coach, parent, spouse, and daughter. So, I decided to start small and build on my successes.

Fewer sharp edges in calls with my mother. Talking to my mother in Canada on the phone, which I do daily, often ends in frustration for me because I worry about her memory deterioration, and I have trouble accepting that she no longer shows up as the mother I experienced growing up. At the same time, I want her to feel safe and loved, not judged.

I used the habit loop to help me improve how I showed up on the phone.

- The cue is calling my mother.
- The craving is that I want to feel supportive of my mother.
- The response is I listen to her without judgment.
- The reward is that I satisfy my craving to be supportive. And listening without judgment becomes associated with a telephone call with my mother.

How did I implement this habit loop? I relied on the "If, then" structure: *If* I am going to call my mother, *then* I will mentally prepare for 60 seconds first. That preparation involves invoking loving feelings, reminding myself of how she must be feeling about her diminished memory, and also focusing on how I'll feel in my body at the end of the call, if it goes well.

I practiced this religiously for a couple of months, approximately 50 times.

What happened? I started to be able to bring up those positive sensations of feeling like a supportive daughter as I started to dial her number. I no longer needed 60 seconds to prepare myself for the call.

Keystone Habits

Keystone habits[11] differ from ordinary habits because they spark chain reactions that launch other good habits. I'm going to cover the four most universal keystone habits that ripple positive change throughout your life—exercise, sleep, meditation, and daily planning.

Keystone habits are an excellent starting point for anyone wanting to bring more positive habits into their life. And they are particularly powerful for folks with ADHD, allowing them to focus on fewer habits, and to easily see the cascading positive behaviors and results that they generate. Identifying a few keystone habits means you don't have to practice dozens of habits to improve your life; rather, you just need to identify a few game changers.

I have one client with ADHD who refers to these four keystone habits as "having all four wheels on the ground each day." I like that image because with four wheels down, you can cover a lot of ground efficiently.

Exercise

Research indicates that regular exercise (at least 3× per week) leads to healthier eating habits, better sleep, increased emotional control, less stress, better mood, and increased productivity at work. A workout is a visible accomplishment that also delivers a tangible dopamine hit that also increases motivation and drive.[12]

Sleep

Sleep is the foundation for an energized, productive day. One study reported that, on average, people who get five to six hours of sleep are 19% less productive than those who get seven to eight hours of sleep per night. Even worse, those who sleep less than five hours per night tend to be 29% less productive.[13]

Though our culture right now (mistakenly) celebrates working with little sleep, negative ripple effects are associated with too little sleep. Research shows lack of sleep leads to fatigue, brain fog, impaired cognitive performance, and low willpower. This leads to unwanted behaviors such as procrastination, lack of focus, and irritability.[14]

Meditation

Meditation is the daily practice of following your breath or focusing on an object or mantra (word or sound) for a period of time, ideally at least 10 minutes. Studies show that your brain physically changes because of meditation. This is called *neuroplasticity*. And this increased neuroplasticity shows up in various parts of the brain, including the amygdala (emotions)[15] and the prefrontal cortex (planning, decision making, and focus).[16] These findings help us understand why regular meditation is linked to a long list of benefits, including less reactivity, reduced stress levels, improved focus, and better decision making.[17]

Daily Planning

Having a plan for the day sets you up to maximize your time, focus on goals, and have a way to measure progress. Intentions are a good starting point, but not enough. Studies have shown that turning an intention into a specific plan makes you 3× more likely to do it (the follow-through rate increased from 34% to 91%). The mere act of planning makes you much more likely to follow through with each activity.[18] For instance, my intention to write this book was noble, but what got it written was a daily plan to write for 60 minutes every morning.

I always reference keystone habits when I start to coach someone who wants to focus on productivity. For someone with ADHD, I start with these four keystone habits and get a sense of if and when these "four wheels" are touching down. Then we tackle them one by one. If I had to recommend one keystone habit to an ADHD client, it would be exercise. A lot of research has been done on the impact of exercise on ADHD symptoms.[19] I have seen time and again that establishing regular exercise habits leads to better sleep, greater ability to handle stress, and more openness to developing better planning skills and tools. The additional benefit of exercise is that even if things go sideways during the day, the sense of accomplishment from having exercised is a true mood booster.

I spend a lot of time with ADHD clients helping them identify the kind of planning and scaffolding that will help them to organize their lives and achieve their goals. For some, that means developing the discipline of lists. For others, the calendar is the key tool for organization and accountability. We know there is no silver bullet. And as mentioned earlier, habit formation is very personal, and that is just as true for folks with ADHD. The keys are patience, the willingness to try different tactics, and accountability for results. And everyone can benefit from a cheerleader—a coach, a family member, or a friend—to help us stay motivated.

We just took a deep dive into habits—what they are and how to develop them. We know that researchers agree upon a few habit best practices, including the power of repetition, starting small, and paying attention to cues, especially your environment. We also know that solidifying your coaching wins can be reinforced through rituals and ongoing learning. Let's dig into those topics next.

Reflection Questions

- Would learning more about how habits are formed help you maintain the positive behaviors you want to solidify for the long run?
- If so, what are some next steps that you could take to learn more about habits (e.g., further reading, webinar, online course, testing out some of the suggestions in this chapter)?
- Which keystone habits could you focus on to put your life on a more positive path?

Resources

- *Atomic Habits* by James Clear, Random House (2018). This book is packed with evidence-based strategies for developing healthy habits. It focuses on teaching how to make small changes that have the power to transform your habits, and ultimately, deliver significant results.

- *The Power of Habits* by Charles Duhigg, Random House (2012). This book explores the science behind habit creation. It explains why habits exist and how they can be changed. His examples from the world of business bring the power of habits to life.

- *The Habit Blueprint: 15 Simple Steps to Transform Your Life* by Patrik Edblad (2016). The author is a certified mental trainer who sets out to answer the question "What are the secrets to lasting change"? He delivers some helpful nuggets and summarizes research from other books very succinctly.

- *Getting Things Done* by David Allen, Penguin Books (2002) is the classic on how to build your own personal productivity system. In many ways it's a time management system. In David's words, "There is an inverse relationship between things on your mind and those things getting done."

- *Tiny Habits: The Small Changes That Change Everything* by BJ Fogg, Ebury Publishing (2020). Another advocate of starting small in order to make lasting change in your life, whether it's losing weight, sleeping more, or restoring your work/life balance.

17

RAM-3, 2, 1: Reinforcing Your Coaching Wins

Continuous effort—not strength or intelligence—is the key to unlocking your potential.

—Winston Churchill

We are always looking for simple hacks to help keep us on track. And while maintaining and reinforcing what you have achieved during coaching requires focus and time, the rewards are enormous. Now that you are on your own, you need tools to keep you focused on your new habits and to not revert back to previous habits.

Not only are you reinforcing thoughts and behaviors that you want to be integral parts of your life, you are also continuing the learning journey. And the brain responds to novelty,[1] so I suggest experimenting with the various strategies in this chapter, picking a couple that work for you and your style, and rotating them from time to time.

RAM-3, 2, 1

This is the mnemonic[2] I created to remind my clients of ways they can reinforce the coaching wins that they have worked so hard to achieve.

3 Rs: Reflection, Recognition, Routines
2 As: Accountability and Accommodation
1 M: Mindset of learning

Reflection

Schedule time to reflect on your coaching progress. This should have a regular cadence, and can be as little as once or twice a month. Some of my clients review their notes and action plans; others keep a journal or a log. The key is to set aside intentional reflection time.

Another takeaway I wish everyone could have: keep a journal beside your bed and write in it either first thing or last thing of the day (or both for the overachievers in the crowd!). I like to have a couple of prompts such as gratitudes, what I did well, what I want to do better, intentions for the day, a daily mantra, and so on. I change my prompts every few months (the brain likes novelty, remember). And sometimes I write lengthy entries about what's going on in my life and my reactions; other times I go through my prompts in a couple of minutes. I find journaling to be enormously powerful because it clears my mind, helps me focus, and has a calming effect.

Here are a few other **reflection hacks**:

- Put a recurring weekly "reflection time" invite into your calendar to serve as a prompt.
- Create a note "Coaching Reflections" on your phone that you add to when you do your weekly planning (an example of habit stacking).

- Ask yourself "How did I do this week?" every Friday as you power down for the weekend.

Recognition

In the previous chapter, I mentioned the power of celebration to reinforce new habits. Let's also remember to celebrate wins. Here are some examples—from big to small—my clients have shared with me.

- A CEO had a celebratory dinner with his spouse after organizing a successful offsite for his leadership team. He specifically carved out time at dinner to share how he had behaved at the offsite (better listening, not jumping in early with his opinions) to make it more successful.
- A CFO who plays "Born in the USA" as his celebratory anthem after financial presentations she feels went well.
- A CMO who keeps a jar of gummy bears in his office, and eats one after meetings when he has asked at least three open-ended questions.

Routines and Rituals

Create rituals or routines to reinforce your coaching results. Common ones range from visual reminders in your office or near your workplace, such as a sticky note with a key message to yourself, to mantras you repeat before challenging work situations. Research[3] has shown that "talking to yourself aloud can motivate you to move forward with your goals, help you focus on a challenging task at hand, and combat self-criticism."[4]

Social psychologist and Harvard business school professor Amy Cuddy's work in this realm is well known, specifically her work on body language. I have a client, Henry, who developed a three-part affirmation during our coaching work together to help deal with his performance anxiety. He calls it "standing up and taking up space" and he repeats it aloud before going into high-pressure meetings.

You deserve to be in this meeting, Henry. You have a lot to contribute, Henry. You've got this, Henry!

Notice that Henry talks to himself in the third person. According to Ethan Kross's book *Chatter*, using your name when you talk to yourself aloud can help you see things from a distance—and that perspective can help reframe negative self-talk and provide some much-needed objectivity and self-compassion.

Other examples of effective routines include regular mindfulness exercises, checklists and playbooks for repeated events and processes, and prioritization systems. I have one client with ADHD, Jose, who sends his three work priorities and self-coaching reminders for the day to his assistant every morning. His assistant follows up at the end of the day by text to check in on progress. Not everyone has access to this level of support, but an easy hack would be to send your list of daily priorities and coaching intentions to yourself each morning and revisit them at the end of the day.

Accountability

Find someone to hold you accountable after the coaching is over. Will your boss play this role? Are there trusted colleagues, friends, or family members who agree to give you feedback if they see you reverting to behaviors you worked hard to change? What about tactics to hold yourself accountable via self-talk?

At least initially, you want this accountability to be frequent and both "in the moment" and scheduled, especially with your boss. The easiest way to do that is to include feedback on your coaching goals as an agenda item in your regularly scheduled one-on-one check-ins.

I often schedule two quarterly check-ins with my clients after our coaching engagements end, and the focus of those check-ins is on how they are maintaining and building on their coaching wins. Often their big ah-ha is when they realize tools and strategies we worked on together are applicable across a spectrum of situations, including their personal lives.

Accommodation

Be kind to yourself, and remember progress isn't linear. If you have a setback and see a backslide, try to refocus on what you have already achieved, and visualize continuing those behaviors. This is where these different strategies intersect. Journaling about what has gone right—and wrong—can be an important act of kindness. Also, use self-talk to remind yourself of all the progress you have made. All those wins are not gone just because you had a setback. Try to reframe the setback as another part of your learning journey. In the words of numerous meditation gurus: *Take a breath and start again, over and over.*

Mindset of Learning

Maintain your curiosity about your personal and professional development journey by seeking out articles, books, blog posts, podcasts, and videos to support it. And remember to set aside time to read, listen, and watch them! This theme runs through this entire book. Curiosity is your best friend. There is so much rich content available that sometimes the problem is deciding what to pay attention to.

I suggest thinking about your preferred style of learning and then finding a few sources for your content. I am an audio learner and I often write notes on my phone while listening to a podcast or audio book. My go-to podcasts focus on neuroscience and leadership, start-ups, classic business sources like *Harvard*

Business Review, and podcasts of coaches and business leaders whom I follow. And once in a while, I will do a random search on a coaching topic I'm interested in to add some variety and different perspectives.

Invoke a Wise Friend

Inevitably, RAM-3, 2, 1 strategies overlap, and this powerful tool incorporates reflection, recognition, accountability, and accommodation.

In situations where you are trying to evaluate how you showed up and demonstrated your coaching progress, try to imagine a discussion with a wise friend. Of course, you can have a real-life conversation, too, but that isn't always feasible at the spur of the moment. I have a particularly wise friend, Catherine, and when I am trying to debrief my behavior in a recent situation, I invoke Catherine and imagine us walking side by side having a conversation. I like her feedback style. She is straightforward, logical, and kind.

I always have these conversations aloud too! Contemporary theories in cognition and the science of learning show how verbalizing your thoughts and feelings through self-talk helps organize them, improves emotional regulation and heightens motivation.[5]

For instance, I felt my team and I could have shown up better prepared at an important client presentation recently. But I was concerned my tone had been too sharp during our team debrief after the presentation. I invoked my wise friend, Catherine, in my mind for a conversation, and she asked me four questions: "What did you do in the team debrief meeting that reflected your hard work on softening your edges? What could you have done to show up with more softness? What is your most important takeaway? Can you check with any of your team to get their perspective?" I answered each of these questions aloud to myself and even had a next step (calling a colleague) by the end. I also felt calmer in my body and mind.

The wise friend you invoke can be whomever you want. It can even be a relative or mentor who has passed. It can be someone you speak to regularly in real life or someone further out in your orbit who you engage with occasionally. For best results, you should have a sense of whose style works for you when seeking accountability and feedback. I respond well to Catherine because of her calm, matter-of-fact tone. I have clients using this strategy who prefer a soft, gentle wise friend who listens and affirms rather than directly probing.

If you want to try this out, spend a little time thinking about which friend you'd like to invoke and visualize them and the qualities you appreciate about this person. Also think about whether you are walking with this friend, talking on the phone, or sitting beside each other. These visualization hacks make the experience deeper.

Putting It into Practice

I have given you a lot of potential tools here, but I don't recommend using them all at once. That would be overload. I suggest starting with one or two strategies and building from there.

Be realistic about which strategies make the most sense for you. For instance, if you know you are not a morning person, a ritual or routine that involves getting up earlier might not be the best starting point. It takes time and patience to figure out what works best for you. Your learning style and daily rhythm are good starting points to navigate through these suggestions.

The coaching journey doesn't end, it just shifts from a focus primarily on the learning to deepening and then maintaining your coaching wins. And remember, don't let a desire for perfection get in the way of achieving the possible!

Reflection Questions

- Which RAM-3, 2, 1 strategy resonates most with you?
- How will you put this strategy into action?
- What might get in the way of you putting it into action? And how can you plan for that possibility?

Resources

- *Chatter: The Voice in Our Head, Why It Matters, and How to Harness It* by Ethan Kross, Crown (2021). I read this book cover to cover after hearing Ethan on a podcast. It focuses on ways to combat negative self-talk and includes an interesting discussion about how it has risen dramatically since social media became so widespread.
- "Your Body Language May Shape Who You Are by Amy Cuddy," *Ted Talk* (2012). This is one of the most watched TED Talks. She suggests tactics for us to feel more powerful in our bodies and convey that to others through our body language.
- *Hardwired for Happiness* by Ashish Kothari (2022). Ashish's deeply researched book is a how-to guide for building the habits and routines in your life that science tells us lead to greater happiness.
- *Mindset: The New Psychology of Success* by Carol Dweck and first published in 2006. This psychologist introduced the world to the phrase *growth mindset*, which has now entered the lexicon of self-help and professional development. This book is a must-read, featuring key insights into redefining success, building lifelong resilience, and supercharging self-improvement.

- *Real Change: Mindfulness to Heal Ourselves and the World* by Sharon Salzberg, Flatiron Books (2020). She is one of the most renowned meditation teachers and authors. This is a guidebook to use meditation to build inner strength and create a better world.

18

Parting Words

The purpose of life is to live it, to taste experience to the utmost, to reach out eagerly and without fear for a newer and richer experience.

—Eleanor Roosevelt

I set out to write a short, funny, pithy how-to guide on coaching yourself. I didn't think it needed to be long because what I wanted to share was straightforward and I pride myself on getting to the point quickly. But as I got deeper into the writing, the book became more ambitious, candid, and, yes, expansive. The content demanded that it be taken seriously and that the book be delivered to you, the reader, with depth and nuance. And my clients' stories needed to be developed so they had enough space to be meaningful.

I hope you found and will continue to find this book to be a helpful and easy-to-use reference guide to support you on your continuing journey of self-discovery. Writing this book was a joyful experience for me. I was able to reacquaint myself with these beloved frameworks, and I found myself using them with even more enthusiasm, and sharing parts of the book with clients when I wanted them to have a takeaway reference relevant to a topic we'd discussed in our sessions.

For me, a good coaching framework lightens the cognitive load, and they can do the same for you. They give you a solid starting point for your journey. That's their beauty. I have introduced every coaching framework in this book to my coaching clients numerous times over the past 10 years. You can now put these coaching frameworks to use in so many different ways:

- Apply them like a recipe, step by step and with precision.
- Mull them over and adapt them in a very loose way, using the elements that best work for you.
- Consider them as reflection tools to help you understand challenges and gain greater awareness about future options open to you.

My hope is that you will use this book often and well, and that the tools and frameworks here will bring you satisfaction, structure, and success as you put them to use.

Get the Most from This Book as You Move Forward

I started the book with suggestions about how to get the most out of this book from a tactical sense. Now I want to share key themes that will help you to implement all the frameworks more successfully. I call them the **5 Ps of Possibility and Progress**.

1. **Practice, practice, practice**. Anything worth achieving takes hard work and repetition. We have all heard this before. So what? It's true. Try new approaches and take calculated risks on your coaching journey. When a new approach leads to an experience you like, practice it over and over.
2. **Patience**. Show yourself some. Change takes time. Be kind to yourself. We stumble, we backtrack, we fall, but if we

are patient with ourselves, we will pick ourselves up and move forward.

3. **Perfection.** Let it go. Don't let the desire for perfection get in the way of the possible. Perfection doesn't exist . . . but incremental improvements make a huge difference, and they deliver compound interest.

4. **Pity parties**. Let's not throw them. Life is tough. Life is challenging. Yes, some people have a harder time than others. Yet, we all can look at a situation and ask ourselves, "What is my agency here? What can I learn from this?" We all have choices and we all have the power to make the best of a situation, if we have the mindset to do so.

5. **Party**. Celebrate. The fact that you have read this book and are focused on personal and professional development is already a reason to celebrate. Change is hard to achieve so please remember to celebrate along the way. And it increases the joy quotient as well.

Final Words

I want to leave you with five key messages that shape this entire book and reinforce why these frameworks are so valuable on your personal coaching journey. They are simple, but not simplistic ideas, and each is easily expressed in a single sentence.

- Cultivate your curiosity by asking thoughtful questions and listening deeply.
- Your coaching is a journey with many insights and learning moments, not a singular destination with total resolution.
- You achieve real success when you cascade your big intentions into measurable goals backstopped by solid habits.
- You are worth every penny you spend on improving yourself. Invest in your mind, body, and soul.

And for my readers with ADHD:

- Stand loud and proud with your neurodiversity; lean into your superpowers and use them well.

Together, we have covered a great deal of ground in this book. I'm curious to know which of the frameworks resonated most with you and which ones you have already put into action or plan to. You can let me know by going on my website and leaving me a note via the contact form. I'd love to hear from you.
Onward!

Appendix 1: Coaching Frameworks at a Glance

Part 2: Coaching Frameworks for Takeoff

Framework	Goal	How do you use this framework?	When do you use it?	Who is involved?[1]
Core Values Framework: Anchor Your Journey (Chapter 5)	Define your North Star and set priorities.	Self-reflect to select your top five values and how to activate them in your actions, speech and plans.	Launch of a coaching engagement. Career transition. At least annually since values change over time.	You
Mind the Gap Framework (Chapter 6)	Determine the focus of your coaching work through understanding what is in the "gap."	Define your current state and the future state you want to achieve. Figure out the issues at play in the gap between these two states.	Diagnosis of a coaching challenge. Launch of a coaching engagement.	You
Spectator-Actor Mindset Framework (Chapter 7)	Reframe a situation so you can see options available to you more clearly.	Analyze a challenge facing you with an actor mindset (What can I control?) instead of a spectator mindset (What is happening to me?).	Launch of a coaching engagement. Day-to-day situations that arise.	You and others involved in the situation that you want to resolve

Part 3: Navigating Challenging Conversations

	Goal	How do you use this framework?	When do you use it?	Who is involved?
Four Key Building Blocks for Critical Conversations (Chapter 8)	Set yourself up for success in all your important communications by incorporating these four fundamentals.	Improve how you apply the four fundamentals of strong communication: preparation, curiosity, deep active listening, and open-ended questions.	Preparation for and use during an important conversation.	You and anyone you want to communicate better with
COIN Framework: How to Have a Critical Conversation (Chapter 9)	Increase the probability that your critical conversation has a successful outcome.	Prepare appropriately for a critical conversation; implement four steps (common purpose, observations, inquiry, next steps) during the difficult conversation.	Preparation and use during a conversation that is causing you significant stress and anxiety.	You and others you want to engage in a critical conversation with

(continued)

	Goal	How do you use this framework?	When do you use it?	Who is involved?
Communicate FOR: A Communication Framework Focused on Relationships (Chapter 10)	Improve relationships by communicating and understanding the feelings and needs of yourself and others.	Reframe how you express yourself, hear others, and resolve conflicts by focusing your awareness on what you are seeing, feeling, needing, and requesting.	The maintenance of the relationship is more important than the actual conflict or achieving a particular outcome. A reflection tool to process a challenging relationship.	You and others you care about deeply
Compassionate Candor Framework (Chapter 11)	Deliver meaningful and empathetic feedback that your direct report can hear and act on.	Use four steps (permission, observation, impact, ask) to deliver compassionate, candid, affirming and constructive feedback.	Regularly. Feedback should be delivered frequently when the stakes are not high.	You and your direct reports or You and your boss or You and your peer
Conversation Funnel Framework (Chapter 12)	Ensure more success in a group conversation by focusing on the context and type of conversation needed.	First determine the stage of a conversation (brainstorm, narrow down options, decision making) to better focus your questioning; use of data, and analysis of options.	A group conversation, specifically when objectives and outcomes may not be clear to everyone.	You and others in a group conversation

Part 4: Unlocking the Keys to Great Management

	Goal	How do you use this framework?	When do you use it?	Who is involved?
Four Keys to Great Management: A Meta-Framework (Chapter 13)	Develop the basic competencies of an efficient and effective manager.	Implement these four building blocks of excellent management: build trust, delegate, give feedback, and coach around performance and career.	Every day, all day long.	Any manager, particularly a new one, and their direct reports
GRPI: A Diagnostic Framework to Unlock Team Needs (Chapter 14)	Diagnose the root of a team's problem accurately.	Understand where your team's challenge resides using GRPI hierarchy: -goals -roles and responsibilities -processes -interpersonal relationships.	Diagnostic tool for managers confronted with team challenges.	Any manager and their team
Six Keys to Unlock the Power of a Strong Team (Chapter 15)	Build a successful, strong leadership team by using these six building blocks.	Identify where your team's key areas for improvement areas are and address them: -psychological safety -productive conflict -decision alignment -accountability -results alignment -purpose.	All the time. This framework and diagnostic is well suited to being launched at an offsite.	Any manager and their team or Any team member wanting insights into building a successful team

Appendix 2: ADHD Resource List

The resources available today for adults and children with ADHD is vast, in fact, a little overwhelming. What follows is a curated list of resources that I know and use. Consider it a starting point for you to do your own research, and develop your own short list of "go to" resources.

Podcasts

- I Have ADHD with Kristen Carder
- ADHD Nerds with Jesse J. Anderson
- Faster Than Normal with Peter Shankman
- Distraction with Dr. Ned Hallowell
- ADDitude ADHD Experts Podcast
- ADHD reWired with Eric Tivers

Apps and Websites

- Llama Life – ADHD time management
- ADHD Online – Diagnosis and treatment
- PSYCOM – ADHD online self-assessment of symptoms and lengthy list of info links
- Friendship Circle – This website has excellent resource lists on a variety of topics of interest to adults and children with ADHD, including productivity apps, support organizations, blogs, and forums to follow.

Associations and Government Resources

- Attention Deficit Disorder Association (add.org). The Attention Deficit Disorder Association provides information, resources, and networking opportunities to help adults with Attention Deficit Hyperactivity Disorder lead better lives.

- Additude.org (additudemag.com). Founded in 1998, *ADDitude* magazine provides clear, accurate, user-friendly information and advice from the leading experts and practitioners in mental health and learning for families and adults living with ADHD and learning disabilities.

- CHADD (chadd.org). It is a national nonprofit organization providing education, advocacy, and support for individuals with ADHD. CHADD also publishes a variety of printed materials to keep members and professionals current on research advances, medications, and treatments affecting individuals with ADHD.

- Centre for ADHD Awareness, Canada (caddac.ca). It is a national, nonprofit, umbrella organization providing leadership in education and advocacy for ADHD organizations and individuals across Canada. CADDAC is committed to increasing the understanding of ADHD, therefore decreasing the stigma of ADHD by providing up-to-date scientific information on ADHD.

- Understood (understood.org). It was established to help those who learn and think differently discover their potentials, take control, find community, and stay on positive paths along each stage of life's journey. The focus is on helping them overcome stigma, a lack of awareness, and an idea of normal that doesn't really exist in order to become self-confident, find meaningful work, and ultimately, thrive.

- LD Online (ldonline.org). It seeks to help children and adults reach their full potential by providing accurate information and advice about learning disabilities and ADHD.

- Totally ADD (totallyadd.com). It was created for adults with ADHD and those affected by it, such as family, employers, health professionals, and so on. Through education, humor, and social interaction, Totally ADD provides the tools and support people need to reduce the fear, shame, and stigma associated with ADHD.

Directories for ADHD Coaches

- CHADD Professional Directory
- Attention Deficit Disorder Association (ADDA) Professional Directory
- ADHD Coaches Organization (ACO) Directory of ADHD Coaches

Key ADHD Books

- Books by Edward Hallowell, including:
  - *Driven to Distraction* (revised) (2011)
  - *Answers to Distraction* (2010)
  - *Driven to Distraction at Work* (2015)
- *ADHD: What Everyone Needs to Know* by Stephen P. Hinshaw and Katherine Ellison (2015)
- *The Queen of Distraction: How Women with ADHD Can Conquer Chaos, Find Focus, and Get More Done* by Terry Matlen, MSW (2014)
- *Women with Attention Deficit Disorder: Embrace Your Differences and Transform* by Sari Solden (2019)
- *Your Brain's Not Broken: Strategies for Navigating Your Emotions and Life with ADHD* by Tamara Rosier (2021)

Meditation Books and Apps

For those looking to start a meditation practice.

- *Wherever You Go, There You Are: Mindfulness Meditation in Everyday Life* by John Kabat-Zinn (1994)
- *Meditation for Beginners* by Jack Kornfield (2008)
- *The Miracle of Mindfulness: An Introduction to the Practice of Meditation* by Thich Nhat Hanh (1999)

All of these meditation sites/apps offer free meditations:

- Tara Brach (https://www.tarabrach.com/guided-meditations)
- Calm (https://www.calm.com/)
- Free Mindfulness Project (https://www.freemindfulness .org/)
- UCLA Meditation (https://www.uclahealth.org/programs/ marc/free-guided-meditations)

Documentaries

- *ADD and Loving It* describes life with ADHD from the poignant perspective of a Canadian comedian and two directors. addrc.org/add-and-loving-it (2009)
- *The Disruptors* hears from many people about their ADHD and takes an immersive look at our approach to ADHD that debunks harmful myths about it. https://disruptorsfilm.com/
- Stacey Machelle – YouTube. She has numerous videos and other resources specifically created for black women with ADHD.
- How ADHD Affects Adults | ADHD – Not Just for Kids. https://www.youtube.com/watch?v=jyUVc0Iteb0 (2018)

Notes

Introduction

1. Roy Atkinson, "A Framework Is a Recipe," HDI, December 2017. https://www.thinkhdi.com/library/supportworld/2017/a-framework-is-a-recipe.aspx

Chapter 1

1. Executive Coaching Survey Summary, Sherpa Coaching, 2020.
2. https://www.verywellmind.com/what-is-a-life-coach-4129726
3. Atul Gawande, "Want to Get Great at Something? Get a Coach," TED Talk, 2019. https://www.ted.com/talks/atul_gawande_want_to_get_great_at_something_get_a_coach?language=en
4. ICF Global Coaching Client Study, 2019.
5. 2009 ICF Global Coaching Study.
6. 2009 ICF Global Coaching Study.
7. "Building a Coaching Culture with Managers and Leaders," Human Capital Institute, 2016.
8. Ashley Strahm, "Do more than survive—thrive in turbulent seasons," betterup.com blog, November 2022.
9. "Organizational Coaching Outcomes: A Comparison of a Practitioner Survey and Key Findings from the Literature" *International Journal of Evidence Based Coaching and Mentoring*, 2018.
10. "Why Business Coaching is Booming," *Forbes*, 2018. https://www.forbes.com/sites/russalanprince/2018/10/08/why-business-coaching-is-booming/?sh=4cf2920d20ff
11. Business Coaching Industry in the US—Market Research Report by IBIS World, June 2022. https://www.ibisworld.com/united-states/market-research-reports/business-coaching-industry/
12. Antonia Bowring, "Should You Invest in a Coach?" *Forbes*, October 2022. https://www.forbes.com/sites/forbescoachescouncil/2022/10/21/should-you-invest-in-a-coach/

Chapter 2

1. N Park and C Peterson, Professional School Counselling, 2008. Journals. sagepub.com. https://scholar.google.com/scholar?q=peterson+2008+positive+psychology&hl=en&as_sdt=0&as_vis=1&oi=scholart

2. Seph Fontane Pennock, "Who is Martin Seligman and What Does He Do?" September 2016. https://positivepsychology.com/who-is-martin-seligman/

3. The VIA Institute Character Strengths assessment is a free survey of character strengths that can give you a better sense of the positive psychology approach to coaching. https://www.viacharacter.org/survey/account/register?gclid=CjwKCAjw3K2XBhAzEiwAmmgrApiYth-kh5_mTFrWF54QLIKpzcZb6ZJh-yprUsA05tAT3V-bKCyG8RoCSBQQAvD_BwE

4. https://www.gallup.com/cliftonstrengths/en/home.aspx?gclid=Cj0KCQjw08aYBhDlARIsAA_gb0f38djKL75_BwcYkzTWvAYae33L8Y6n-4Btlfr_h8s8sH8d1QJVHycaAmdSEALw_wcB

Chapter 3

1. "Attention-Deficit/Hyperactivity Disorder," NIH. https://www.nimh.nih.gov/health/topics/attention-deficit-hyperactivity-disorder-adhd

2. The classic with a thorough overview of ADHD is *Driven to Distraction* by Edward Hallowell and John Ratey, 2011.

3. https://www.mountsinai.org/health-library/diseases-conditions/asperger-syndrome

4. Visit the CDC website for the DSM-5 Criteria for ADHD at https://www.cdc.gov/ncbddd/adhd/facts.html

5. ADHD Online (https://adhdonline.com) is a highly regarded site that offers online ADHD assessments. You can visit Psycom at https://www.psycom.net/adhd-test for a simple self- assessment of ADHD symptoms, but it is not a diagnostic test.

6. "Famous People with ADHD", MentalUP. https://www.mentalup.co/blog/famous-people-and-celebrities-with-adhd

7. ADHD coach directories include Attention Deficit Disorder Association (ADDA) Professional Directory, ADHD Coaches Organization (ACO) Directory of ADHD Coaches, and Children and Adults with Attention-Deficit/Hyperactivity Disorder (CHADD) Professional Directory.

Chapter 4

1. Suan Dynarski, "For Note Taking, Low-Tech Is Often Best," Harvard Graduate School of Education, August 2017. https://www.gse.harvard.edu/news/uk/17/08/note-taking-low-tech-often-best

Chapter 5

1. Brene Brown, "Dare to Lead List of Values." https://brenebrown.com/resources/dare-to-lead-list-of-values/

Chapter 6

1. https://www.gse.harvard.edu/news/uk/17/08/note-taking-low-tech-often-best

Chapter 8

1. Robin Abrahams and Boris Groysberg, "How to Become a Better Listener," *Harvard Business Review*, December 2021. https://hbr.org/2021/12/how-to-become-a-better-listener.
2. Nick Morgan, *Power Cues: The Subtle Science of Leading Groups, Persuading Others, and Maximizing Your Personal Impact*, 2014.
3. https://www.gse.harvard.edu/news/uk/17/08/note-taking-low-tech-often-best

Chapter 9

1. I was privileged to work as a facilitator for a company that used this framework as the core of one of its learning modules, and participants loved it. It was always the most highly rated module.
2. For a deep dive into whether you tend toward "soft" or "hard" when you are preparing for a critical conversation that you anticipate will be conflictual, the Thomas-Kilmann Conflict Mode Instrument may be helpful. It is an online assessment focused on two underlying dimensions of human behavior (assertiveness and cooperativeness) and uses them to define five different modes for responding to conflict situations: competing, collaborating, compromising, avoiding, accommodating. We are all capable of using all five modes, the assessment helps measure which ones you tend to rely on and in which settings.

Chapter 10

1. Rosenberg, 2015.

Chapter 11

1. Diane Musho Hamilton, "Calming Your Brain during Conflict," *Harvard Business Review*, December 2015. https://hbr.org/2015/12/calming-your-brain-during-conflict

2. In the second edition of *Radical Candor*, Kim Scott recommends that people use the phrase *compassionate candor* instead of *radical candor*.

3. "Leadership IQ Has a Helpful Online Questionnaire to Gauge Motivation." https://www.leadershipiq.com/blogs/leadershipiq/what-motivates-you

4. "Episode 4: Friends and Foes: The Neuroscience of In-Group and Out-Group with Harvard Professor Dr. Jason Mitchell." Your Brain At Work (That is the name of the NeuroLeadership Institute's podcast), July 2021. https://neuroleadership.com/podcast/neuroscience-of-ingroup-outgroup-jason-mitchell/

Chapter 13

1. Robert Half, "What Is the Difference between a Leader and a Manager?" https://www.roberthalf.jp/en/management-advice/leadership/leader

2. www.manager-tools.com is a vast resource for managers looking for strategies, skills, and tools to be effective on the job.

3. For example, Lattice is a widely used HR platform where you can manage everything from performance reviews to professional development.

4. "The Essentials: Giving Feedback, Women at Work," *Harvard Business Review*, May 2021. https://hbr.org/podcast/2021/05/the-essentials-giving-feedback

5. "Taking Tough Feedback," Mellody Hobson interview, Worklife with Adam Grant, June 2021.

6. Dan McCarthy, "70 Coaching Questions for Managers Using the GROW Model," November 2019. www.liveabout.com; For managers, a lengthy list of open-ended questions for coaching reportees. The questions are organized around the GROW Model, May 2023. https://www.the coachingtoolscompany.com/the-grow-model-explainedfor-coaches-questions-tips-more/

7. Chapter 7, "Getting Results with Effective Collaboration," *Radical Candor* (2017) by Kim Scott is devoted entirely to career coaching conversations between managers and direct reports and is well worth the read. She credits her business partner, Russ Laraway, with developing this process.

Chapter 14

1. "The GRPI Model of Team Effectiveness: Explained," Academy to Innovate HR (AIHR). https://www.aihr.com/blog/grpi-model/#What
2. https://www.coursehero.com/file/75749704/GRPI-MODELpdf/

Chapter 15

1. William Kahn, "Psychological Conditions of Personal Engagement and Disengagement at Work," *Academy of Management Journal*, 1990, 33(4): 692–724.
2. Dr. Jacinta Jimenez, "Why psychological safety matters at work and how to create it," Betterup.com Blog, October 2022. https://www.betterup .com/blog/why-psychological-safety-at-work-matters
3. Patrick Lencioni, *The Advantage*, Chapter 3, "Discipline 1: Build a Cohesive Leadership Team," 2012.

Chapter 16

1. David T. Neal, Wendy Wood, and Jeffery M. Quinn, "Habits—A Repeat Performance" *Current Directions in Psychological Science* 2006, 15(4): 198–202. web.archive.org/web/20110526144503/http:/dornsife.usc.edu/ wendywood/research/documents/Neal. Wood. Quinn.2006.pdf
2. Clear, *Atomic Habits*, p. 19.
3. Ann M. Graybiel, "The Basal Ganglia and Chunking of Action Repertoires," *Neurobiology of Learning and Memory*, 1998, 70: 119–136. https://news.mit.edu/1999/habits
4. Fogg, *Tiny Habits*, p. 134.
5. Fogg, *Tiny Habits*, p. 10.
6. Cameron Huddleston, "How much you'd have if you saved $1 a day for the rest of your life," *Business Insider*, July 2017.

https://www.businessinsider.com/how-much-youd-have-if-you-saved-1-a-day-for-the-rest-of-your-life-2017-7.

7. Clear, *Atomic Habits*, p. 15.

8. Dr. Peter Vishton, "Reigning in Your Inner Child: Better Eating Habits," March 2020. https://www.wondriumdaily.com/reigning-in-your-inner--(obese)-child:-better-eating-habits/

9. "What Vietnam Taught Us about Breaking Bad Habits," NPR, January 2, 2012. https://www.npr.org/sections/health-shots/2012/01/02/144431794/what-vietnam-taught-us-about-breaking-bad-habits

10. Frank Martela, "Autonomy, Competence, Relatedness, and Beneficence: A Multicultural Comparison of the Four Pathways to Meaningful Work," July 2018, *Frontiers of Psychology*, July 2018. https://www.frontiersin.org/articles/10.3389/fpsyg.2018.01157/full

11. This term was coined by Charles Duhigg, *The Power of Habit*.

12. "Longitudinal Gains in Self-Regulation from Regular Physical Exercise," National Library of Medicine, November 2006. https://pubmed.ncbi.nlm.nih.gov/17032494/

13. "Sleep Deprivation: Impact on Cognitive Performance," National Library of Medicine, October 2007. https://www.ncbi.nlm.nih.gov/pmc/articles/PMC2656292/

    "The Link between Sleep and Job Performance," Sleep Foundation. https://www.sleepfoundation.org/sleep-hygiene/good-sleep-and-job-performance

14. "Sleep Deprivation: Impact on Cognitive Performance," National Library of Medicine, October 2007. https://www.ncbi.nlm.nih.gov/pmc/articles/PMC2656292/The Link between Sleep and Job Performance; https://www.sleepfoundation.org/sleep-hygiene/good-sleep-and-job-performance

15. Melissa Conrad Stoppler, "Meditation, Stress and Your Health," Web MD, July 2020. https://www.webmd.com/balance/guide/meditation-natural-remedy-for-insomnia

16. Britta Holzel et al., "Mindfulness practice leads to increases in regional brain gray matter density," *Psychiatry Research*, 2011, 191(1): 36–43. https://www.ncbi.nlm.nih.gov/pmc/articles/PMC3004979/

17. Press release, "Mindfulness meditation training changes brain structure in eight weeks," *Science News*, January 2011. https://www.sciencedaily.com/releases/2011/01/110121144007.htm

18. "Beyond Good Intentions: Prompting People to Make Plans Improves Follow-Through on Important Tasks," Behavioral Science and Policy, December 2015. https://scholar.harvard.edu/files/todd_rogers/files/beyond_good.pdf

19. "The Effects of Physical Exercise on Functional Outcomes in the Treatment of ADHD: A Meta-Analysis," National Library of Medicine, February 2016. https://pubmed.ncbi.nlm.nih.gov/26861158/

Chapter 17

1. "Novelty Improves the Formation and Persistence of Memory in a Naturalistic School Scenario," *Frontiers in Psychology*, 2020. https://www.ncbi.nlm.nih.gov/pmc/articles/PMC7000375/
"Pure Novelty Spurs the Brain," *Science Daily*, 2006. https://www.sciencedaily.com/releases/2006/08/060826180547.htm
2. A mnemonic is defined as "something such as a very short poem or a special word used to help a person remember something." For example, the mnemonic *EADGBE—Elephants and Donkeys Grow Big Ears* is useful for remembering the strings of a guitar in proper order from left to right. https://dictionary.cambridge.org/us/dictionary/english/mnemonic
3. Martha Tesema, "4 Science-Backed Reasons to Say Your Self-Talk Out Loud," May 2021. https://advice.theshineapp.com/articles/4-science-backed-reasons-to-take-your-self-talk-out-loud/.
4. Emma Seppala, "How to Lighten Up on that Daily Self Critique," November 2017. https://advice.theshineapp.com/articles/how-to-let-up-on-that-daily-self-critique/?utm_source=Shine&utm_medium=Blog.
5. Antonia Bowring, "Try Talking to Yourself to Improve Your Performance," *Forbes*, March 2022. https://www.forbes.com/sites/forbescoachescouncil/2022/03/24/try-talking-to-yourself-to-improve-your-performance/.

Appendix 1

1. In the final column "Who is involved?", I did not list any third parties (e.g., coach, therapist, mentor, friend, etc.) who may support you in your coaching work. The "Who" column refers to who might be involved in the application of the framework to your challenge/situation.

Acknowledgments

Joanne Killmeyer and Terry Hogan were my teachers and mentors, and critical in helping me get started as a coach. I hope I can pay it forward and gift to others what they gave to me. While Joanne is no longer with us in body, her spirit continues to inspire many and her work lives on through her students. I miss her always.

Some of the ideas and passages here originally appeared in articles I authored for Forbes, as a member of the Forbes Coaching Council (https://councils.forbes.com/forbescoachescouncil). I appreciate its top-notch editors and the platform's reach.

And the team from Wiley gave me my author cred! Thank you, Victoria Savanh, who believed I had a book in me. Julie Kerr, my patient and supportive editor, always held me to a high standard in a loving way. And the rest of the Wiley team – always ready to answer my questions. Special shout out to Sangeetha and Michelle!

The book benefited greatly from the keen eye of Laura Fromm, my personal editor, who started with me at the beginning and helped me create structure from chaos. Gratitude also to Sarah Allison and Pati Canseco for graphic brilliance.

My marketing team from Eminence, Maria Rosati and Julie Tyler, and the PR team from Smith Publicity have all helped me navigate a very foreign world with encouragement and good humor. Debbie Tomkins is in a class of her own. She keeps me sane and organized and has endless patience. Emma Gershon, for her savvy perspective and "can-do" attitude.

And having these impressive, generous, kind endorsers was a boost of confidence, for sure! It is a gift that keeps giving. Deep thanks to Chris Anderson, Arthur C. Brooks, Christina Tosi, Sally Susman, Alex Chung, Andrew Fingerman, Sarah Slusser, Kerry Sulkowicz, Khe Hy, Lindsay Kaplan, and Pat Mitchell.

A long and loving list of sensational and skilled colleagues supported me from the beginning, including Joanne Heyman, Michelle Friedman, Julie Kantor, Stacy Martin, Mary Stephenson, Nikki Goldman, Alexandra Phillips, Lisa Rubin, Beverly Wallace, Gilly Weinstein, Starla Sireno.

A generous community provided me with encouragement and invaluable insights along the way. Specific shout-outs to Anita, Bridgit and Anisha at Chief, Cat Colella-Graham, Ellen Archer, Cookie Boyle, Jennie Glazer, Jen Mormile, Taryn Langer, Jen Mirsky, Adam Reingold, Melanie Pitson, Laura Yorke, Vik Kapoor, Lisa Shreve, Reagan Walsh, Felipe Propper de Callejon and Holly Youngwood.

Many clients contributed their personal stories to this book, and I am grateful to all of them for sharing their work and life experiences with me. They are, to a one, a pleasure to work with and without them, this book would not have been possible. I feel blessed to work with all of them. A special shout out to Steven and James, they know why.

Finally, I'm deeply grateful to my family—Diana, Luca, and Ale—for their humor, love and support. Luca gets an extra nod because his ADHD journey was the impetus for mine, and that has been a true gift.

About the Author

Antonia Bowring is a highly credentialed, top New York executive coach. She works with founders, C-Suite executives, and leadership teams. One of Antonia's areas of expertise is helping neurodiverse leaders create the necessary scaffolding to leverage their gifts and maintain their focus.

She is a frequent speaker to companies and groups on topics ranging from the leadership mindset to ADHD in the workplace to communication best practices. Her articles through the Forbes Coaches Council are widely read, and *The American Reporter* named her one of the 10 leadership coaches to watch in 2022.

She is passionate about her work, her family, and endurance fitness challenges: next up is a 515-mile solo trek on the Northern Route of the Camino de Santiago in Spain. She lives in New York City, but British Columbia is home in her heart. Find out more about Antonia at ab-strategies.com (www.ab-strategies.com/).

Index